Faces of the World

Designs to Inspire Your Creative Genius

Published in 2015 by Global Insight Productions

Illustrators Ewelina Terczynska, Doyle, and Surabhi

Creative Director Rosa MeChel

www.BeHappyColoringBooks.com

ISBN: 978-0-9796942-9-5

Join Our Creative Community
BeHappyColoringBooks.com

For your coloring and painting pleasure,
if you have creative genius ideas that you
would like for our artist to design, let us know.

We also want you to be a part of our Be Happy
Art Gallery. So go ahead and send us your
masterpiece and we will share it with the world.

You can contact us at **info@behappycoloring.com**

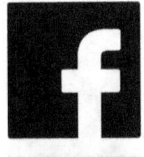 facebook.com/behappycoloring

 pinterest.com/behappycoloring

 Instagram.com/behappycoloring

 twitter.com/behappycoloring

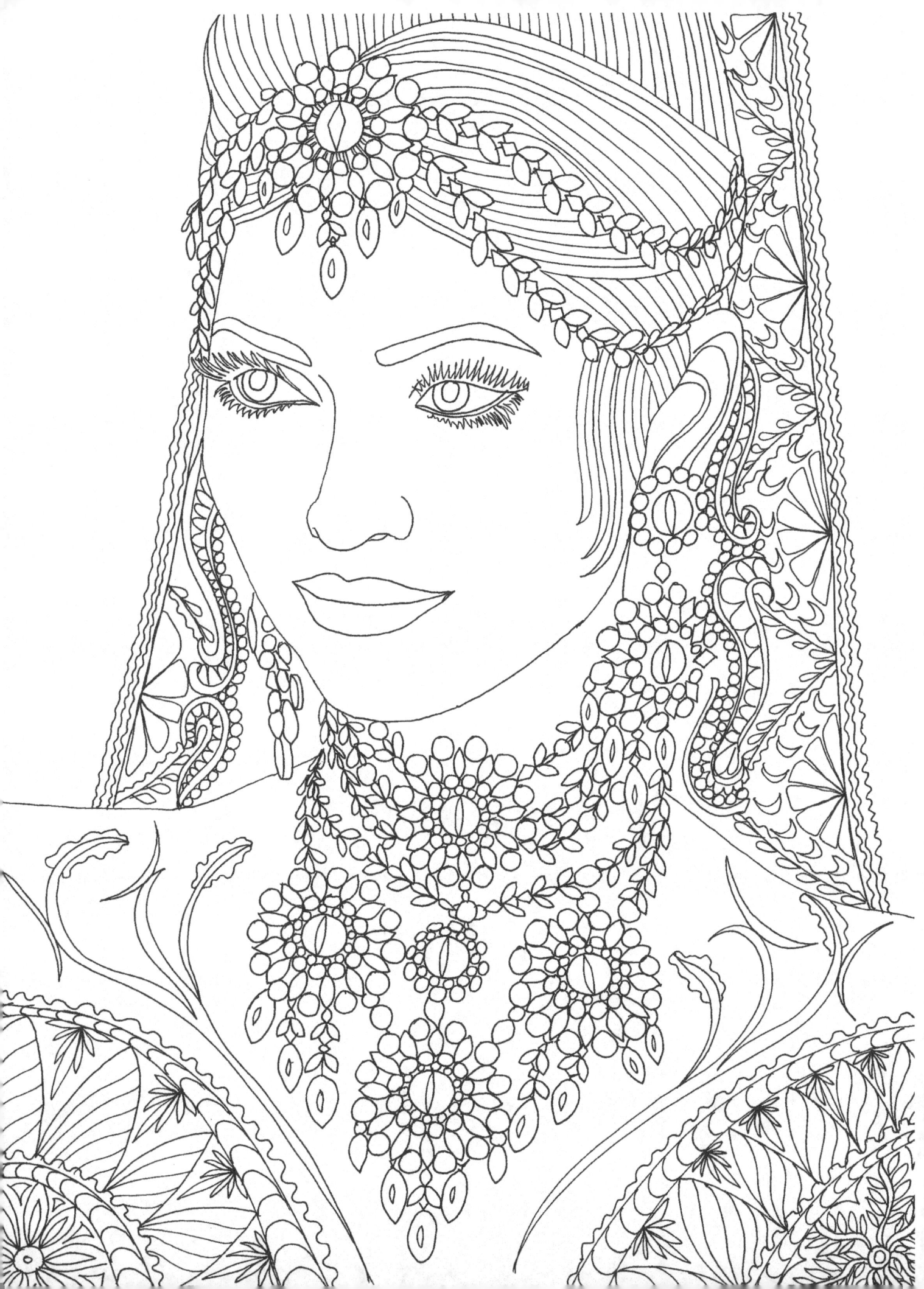

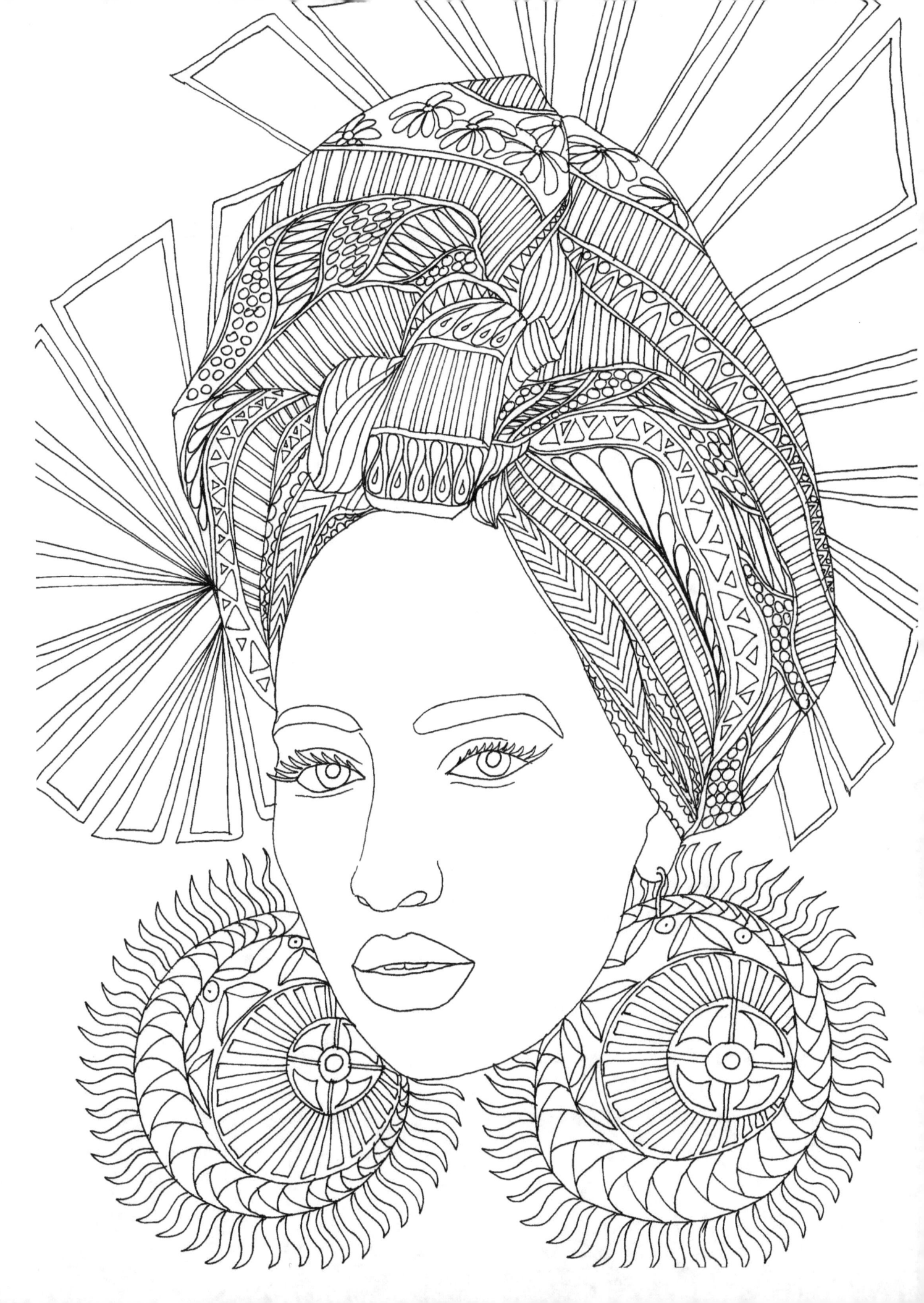

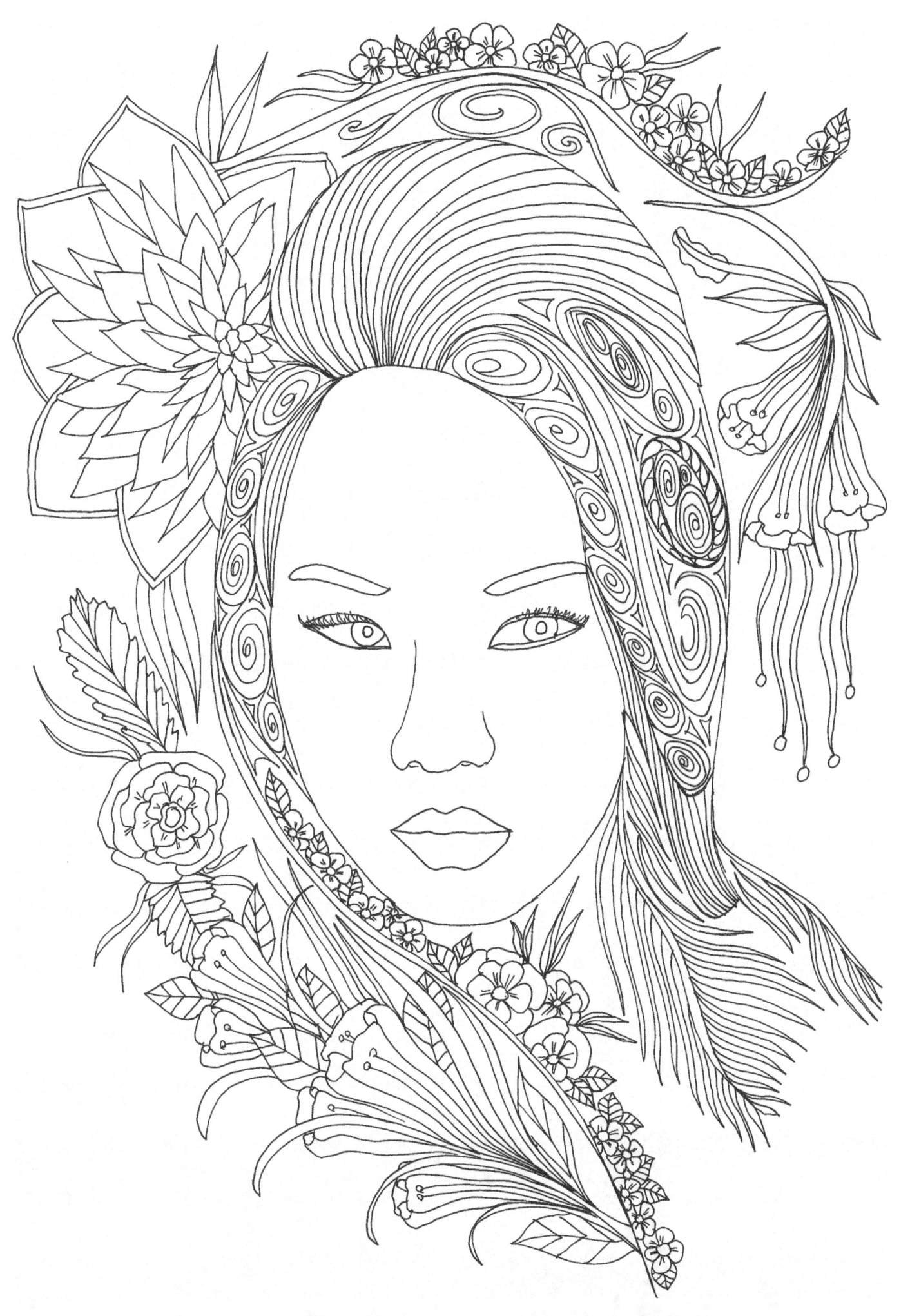

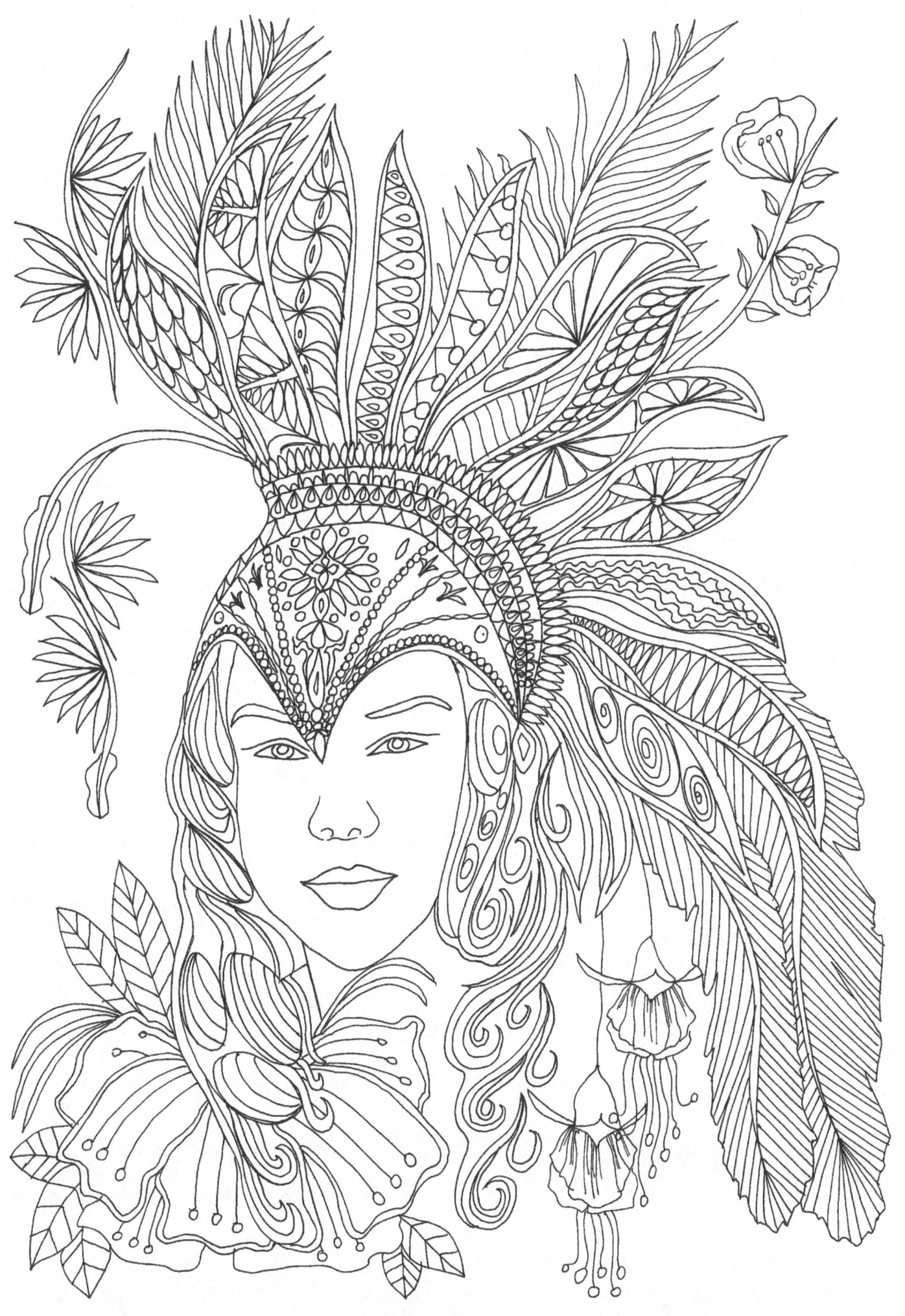

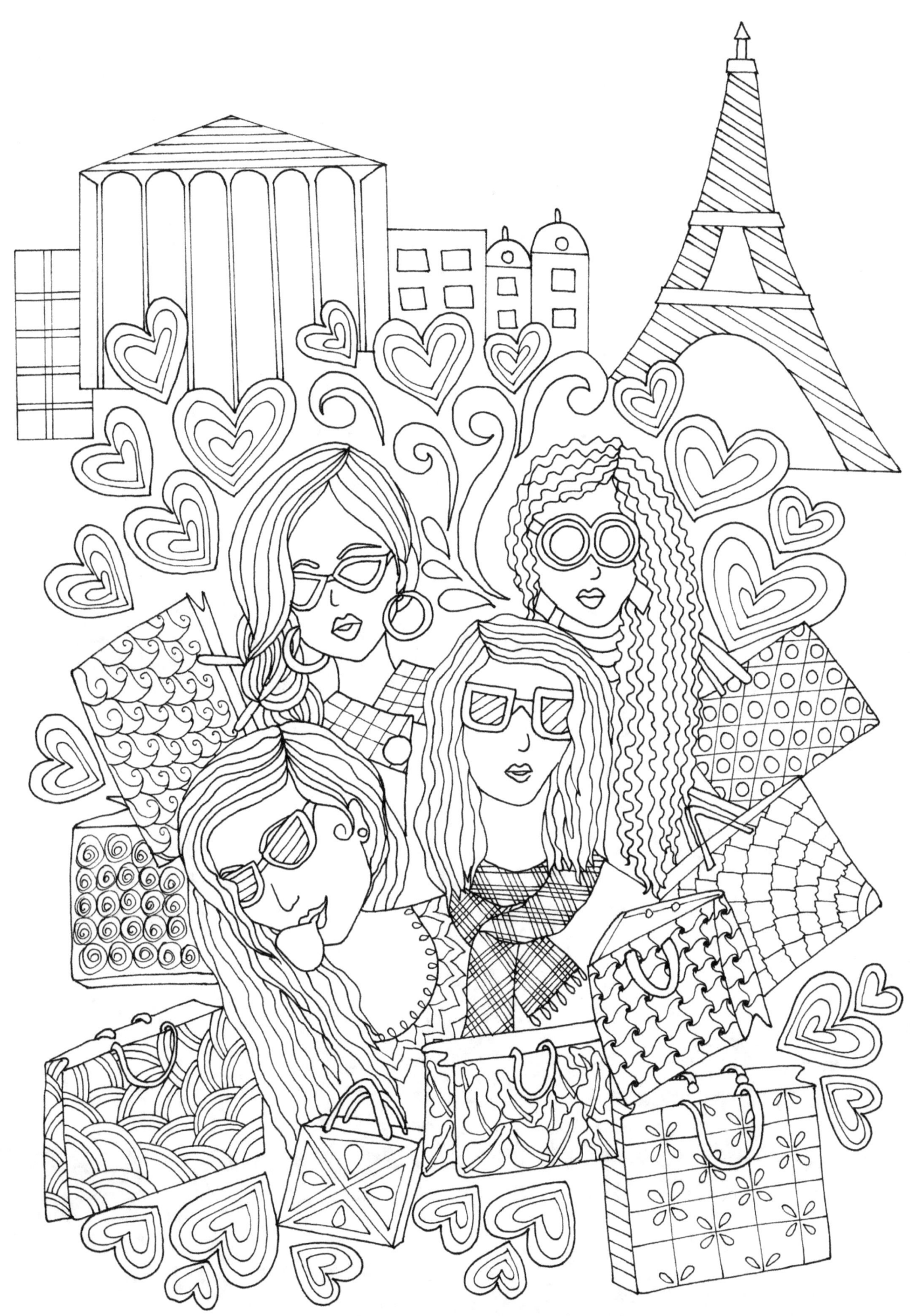

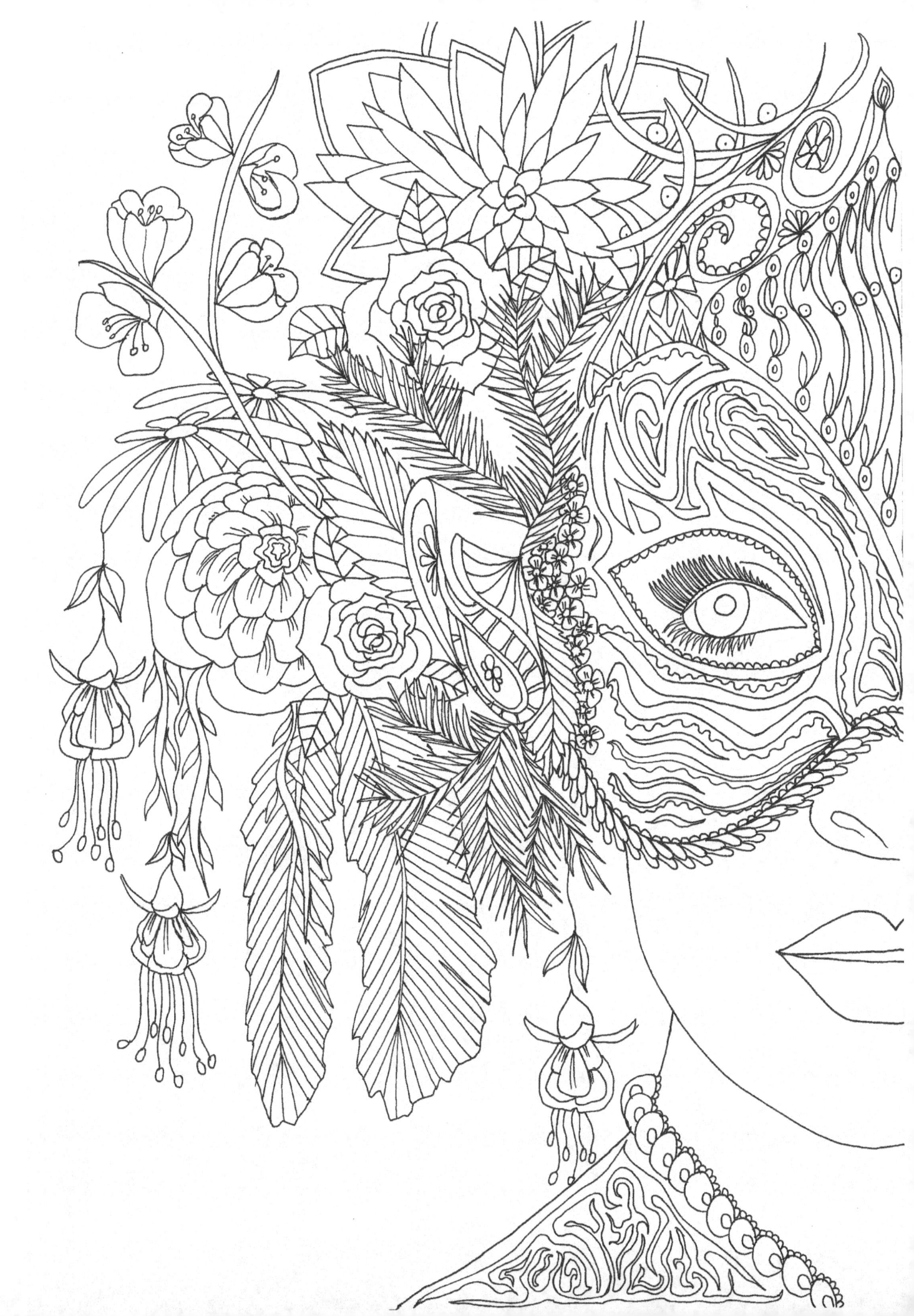

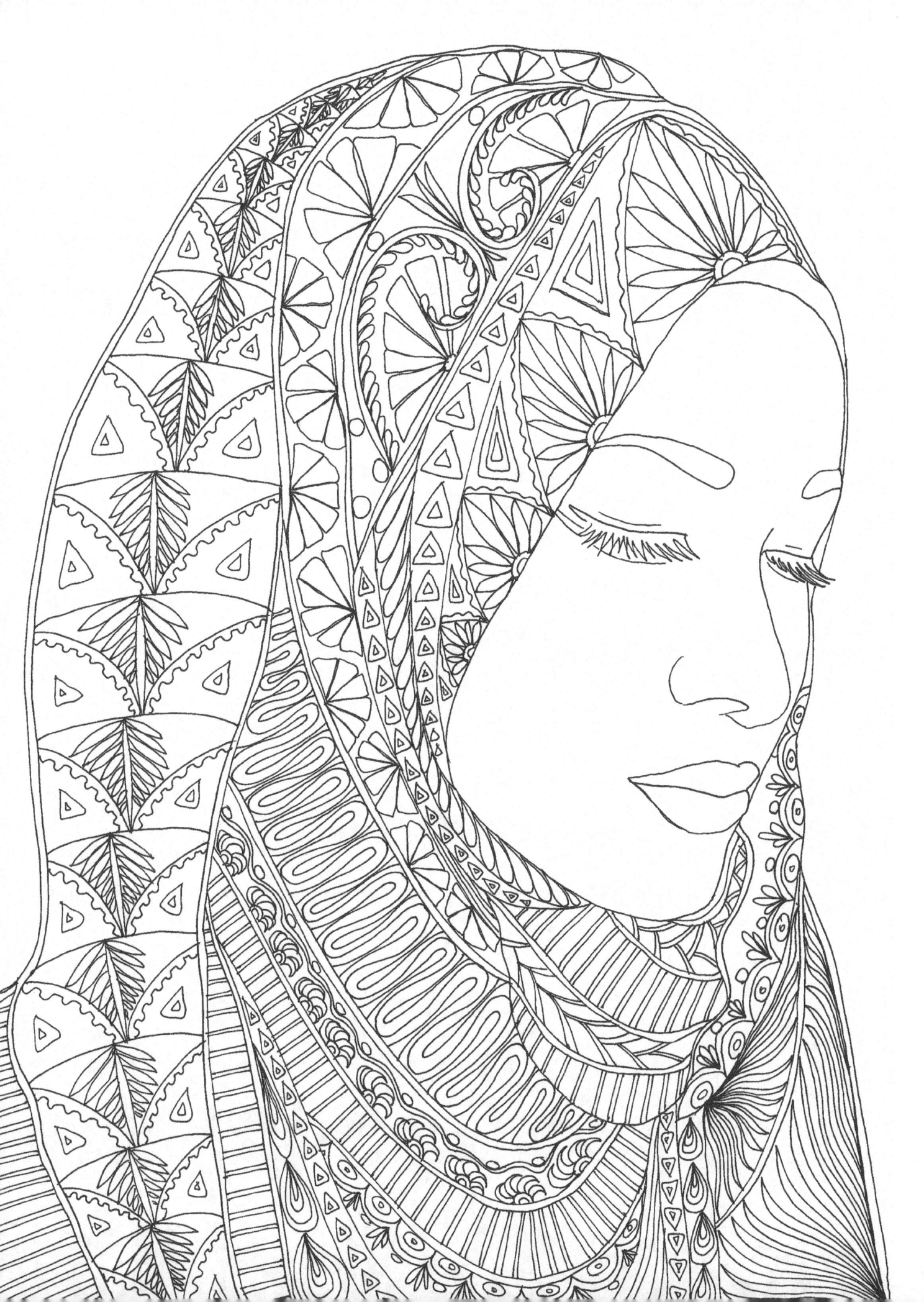

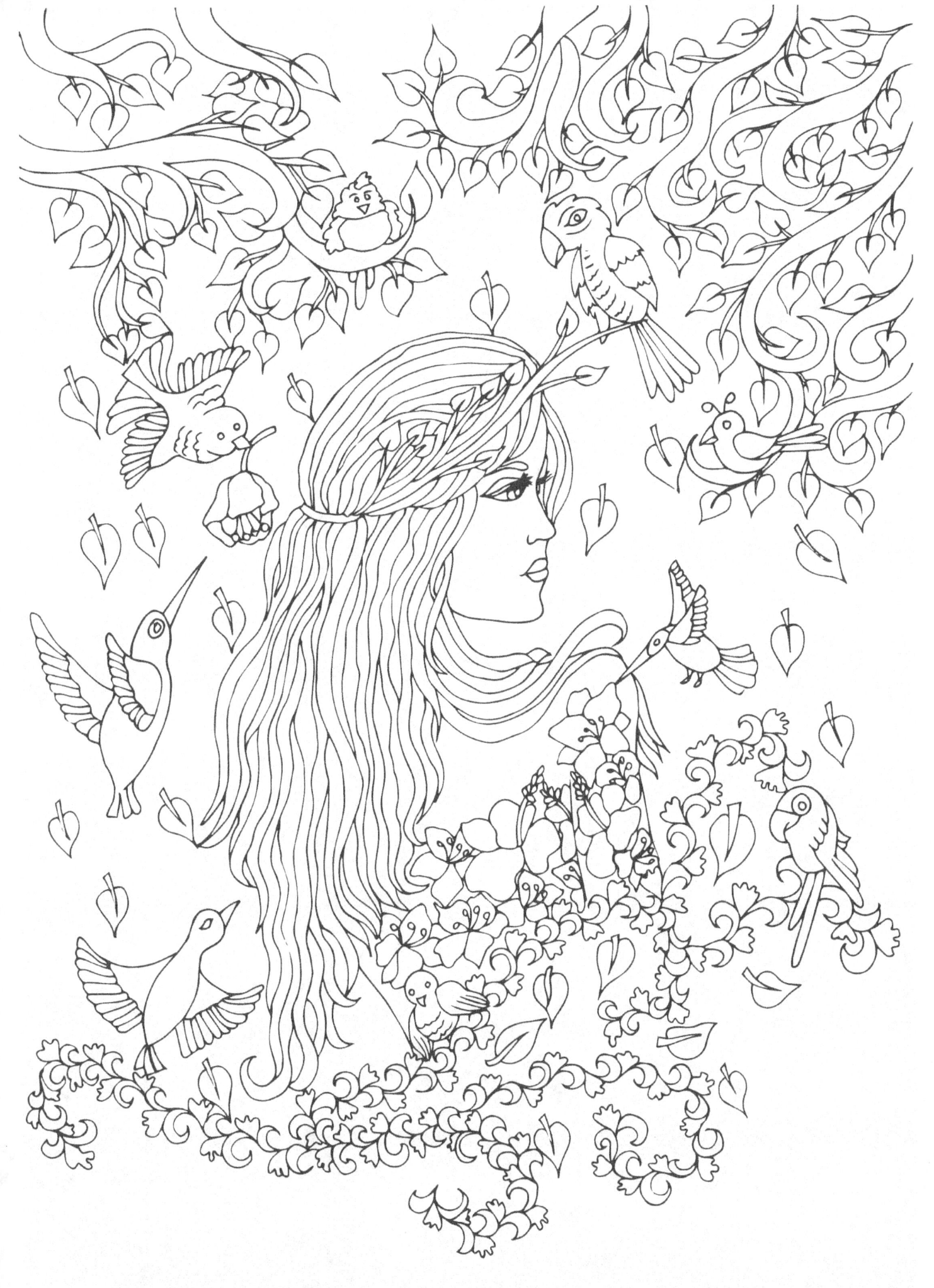

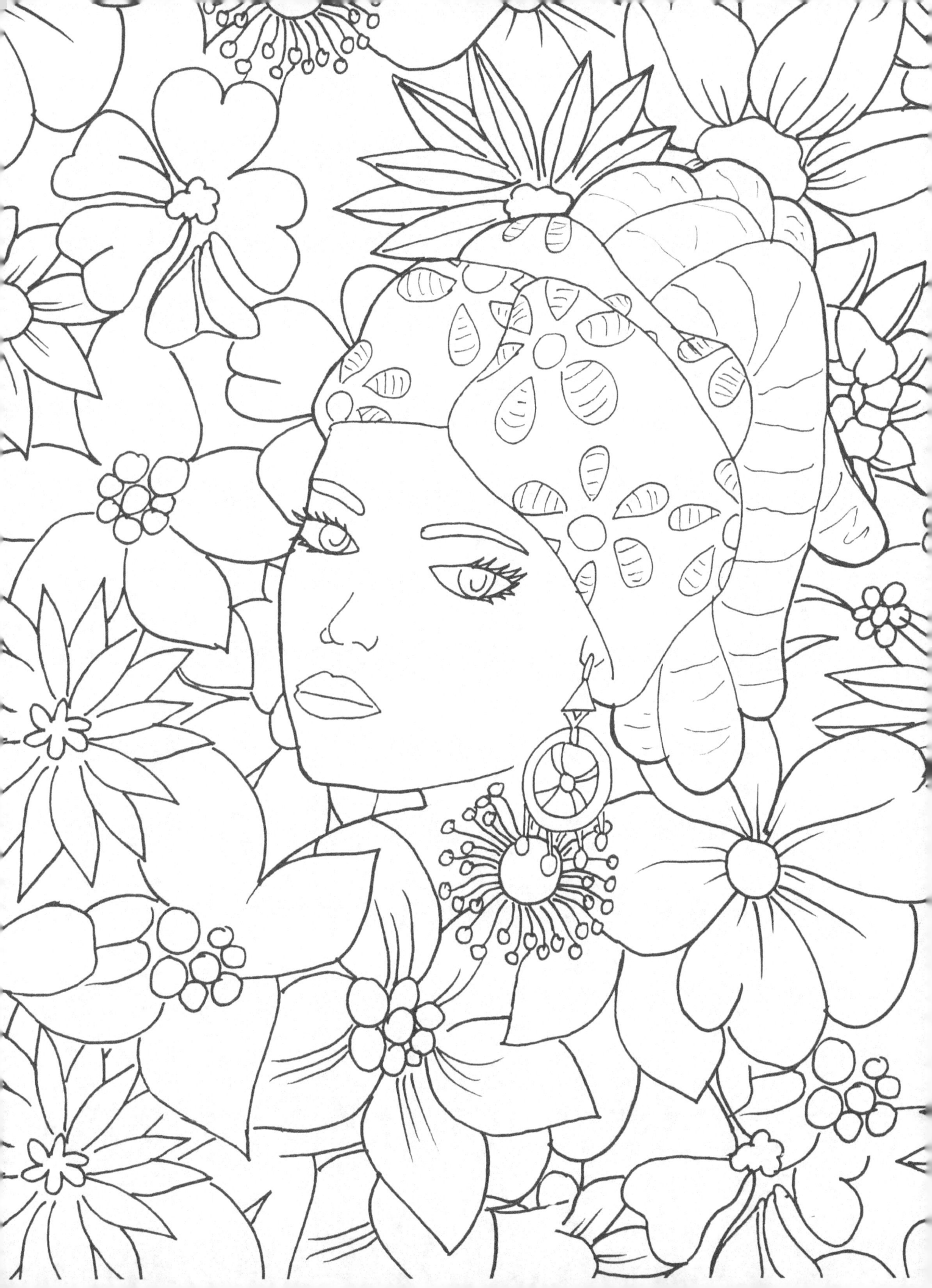

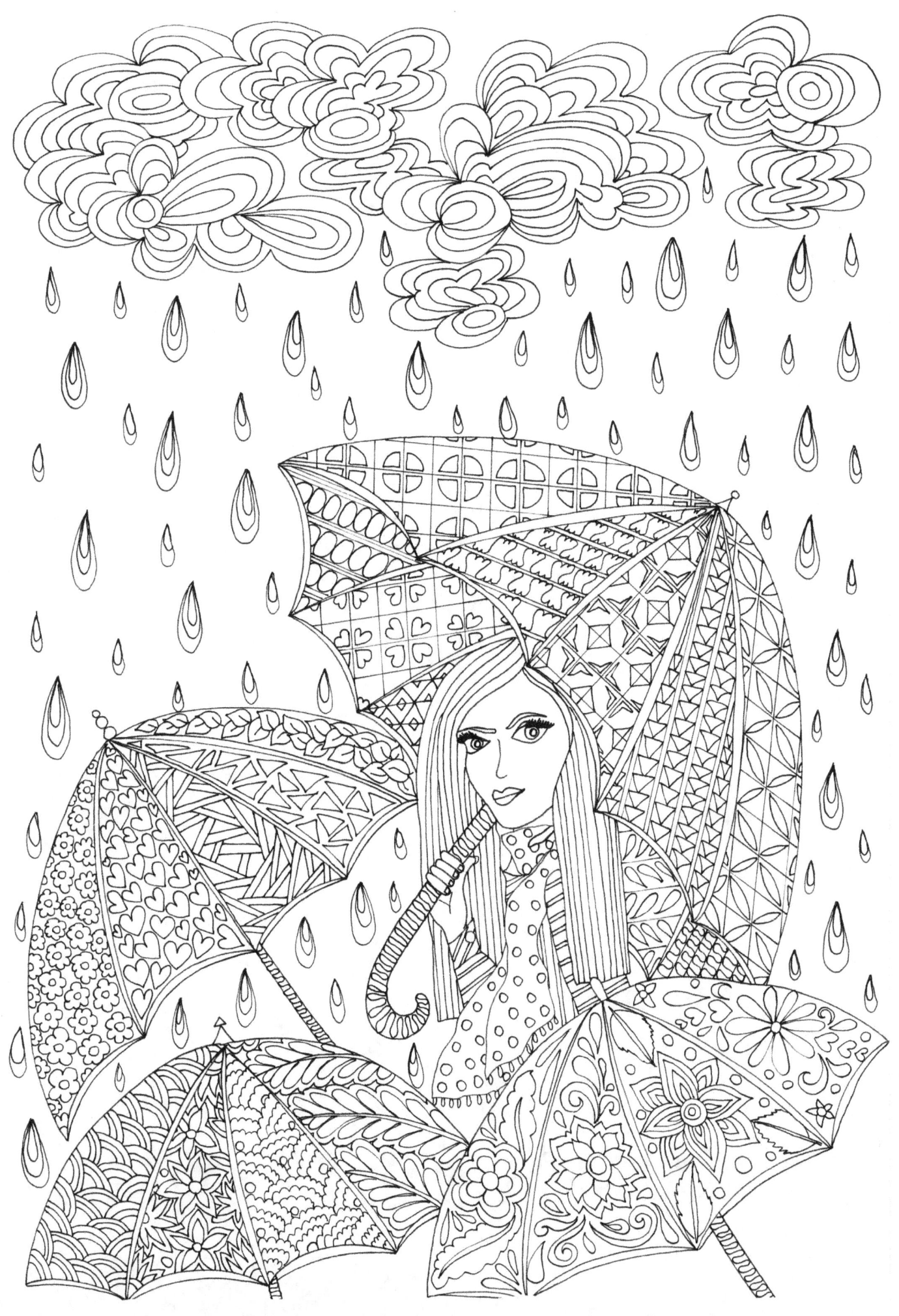

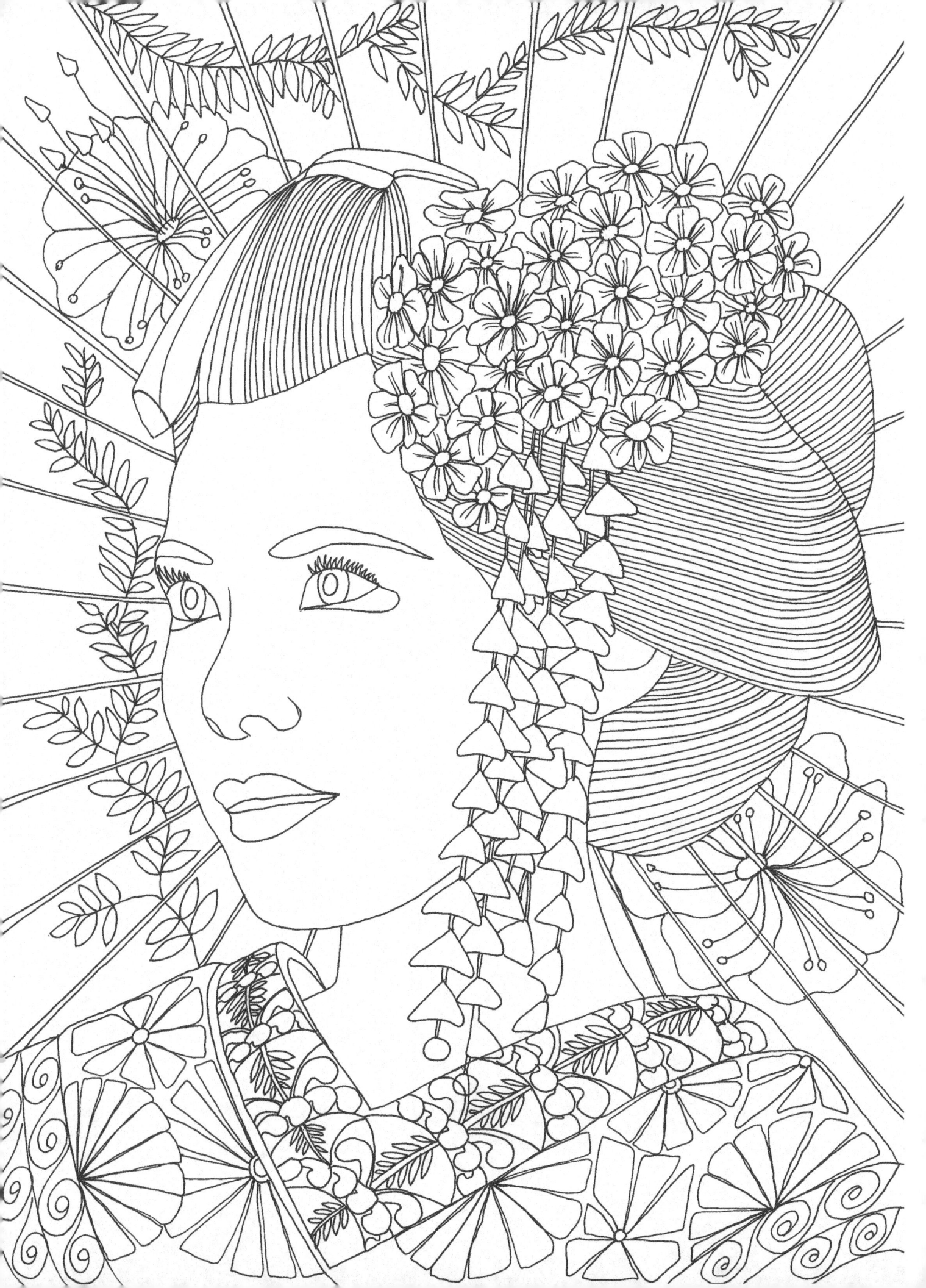

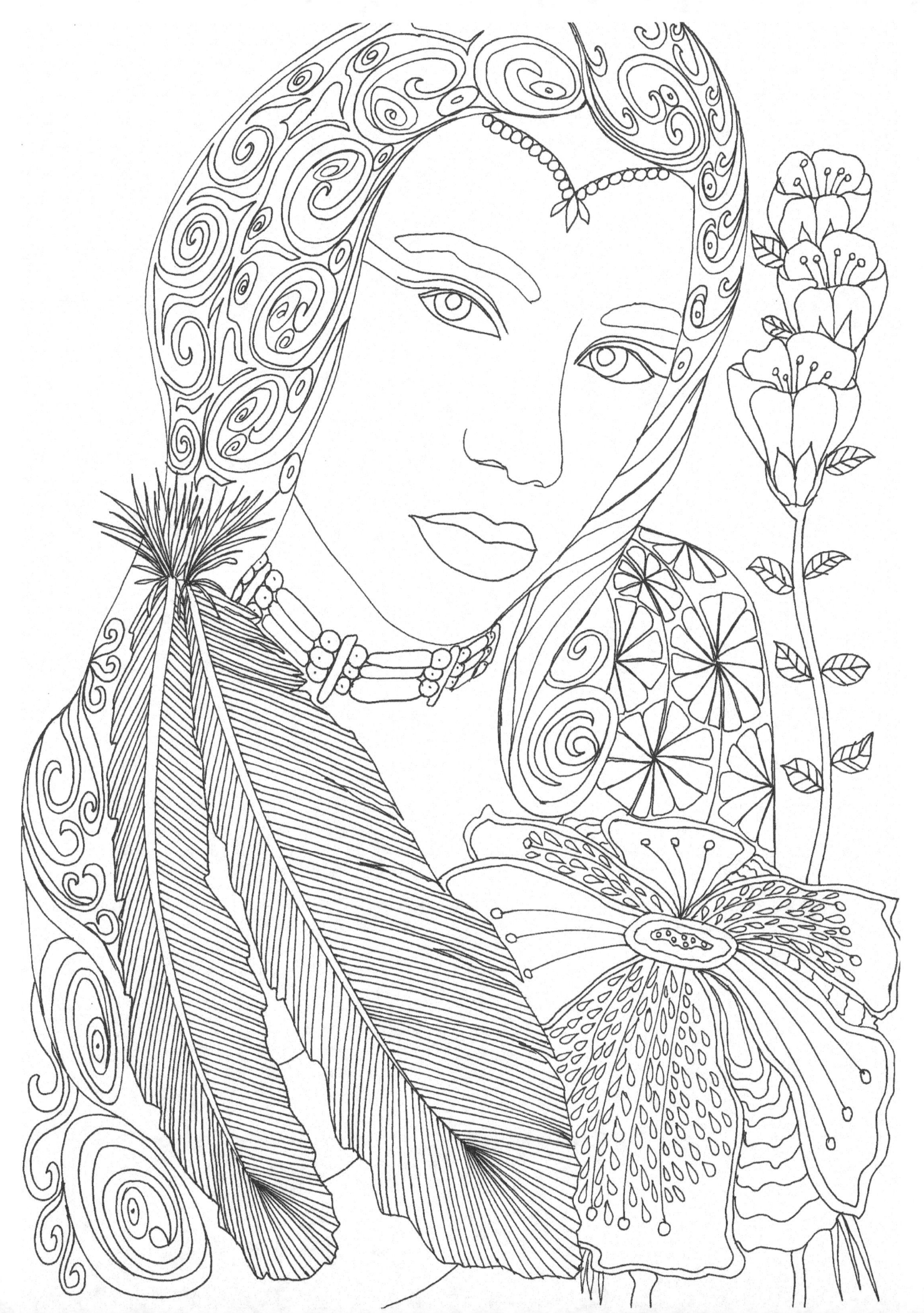

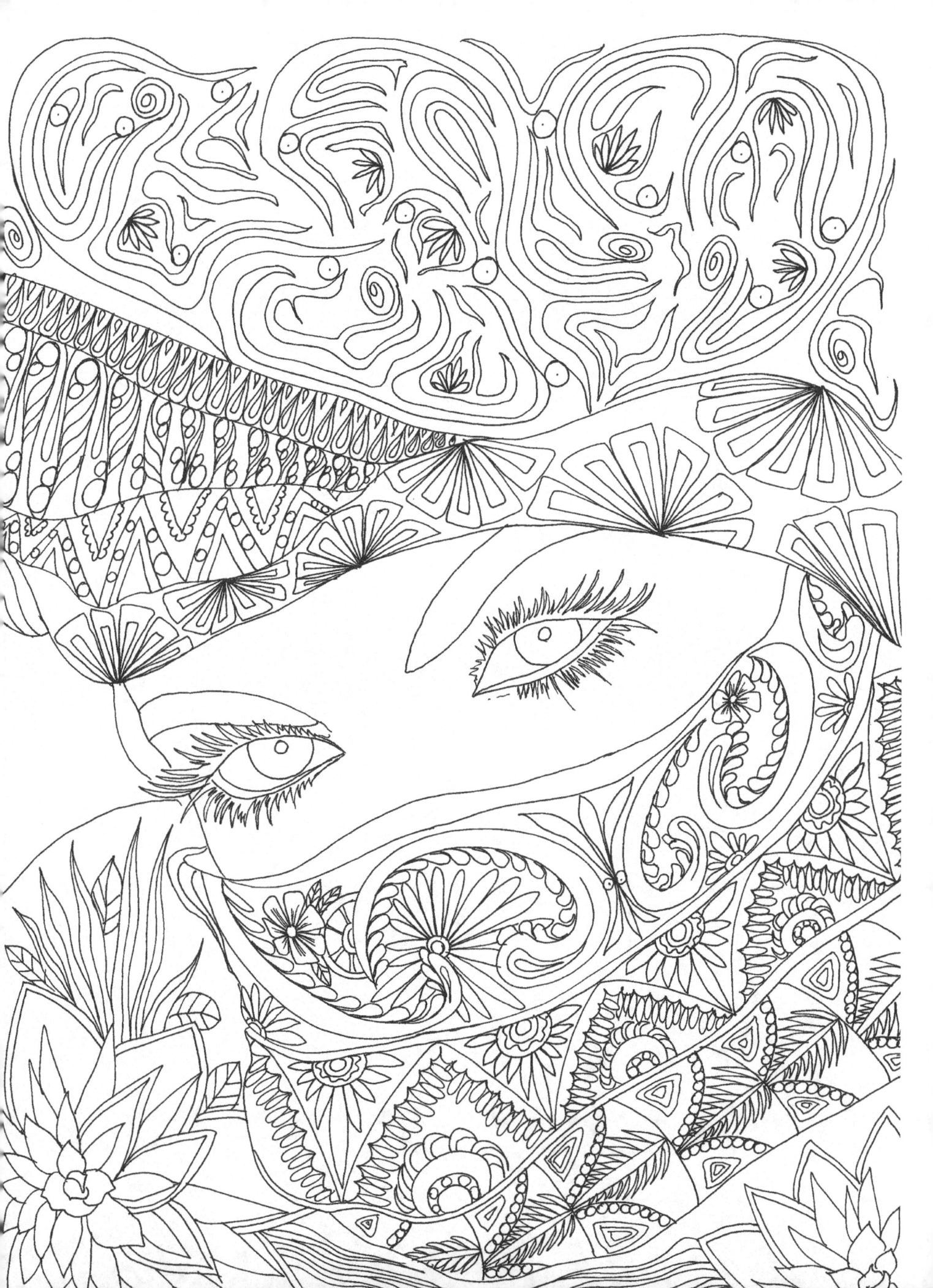

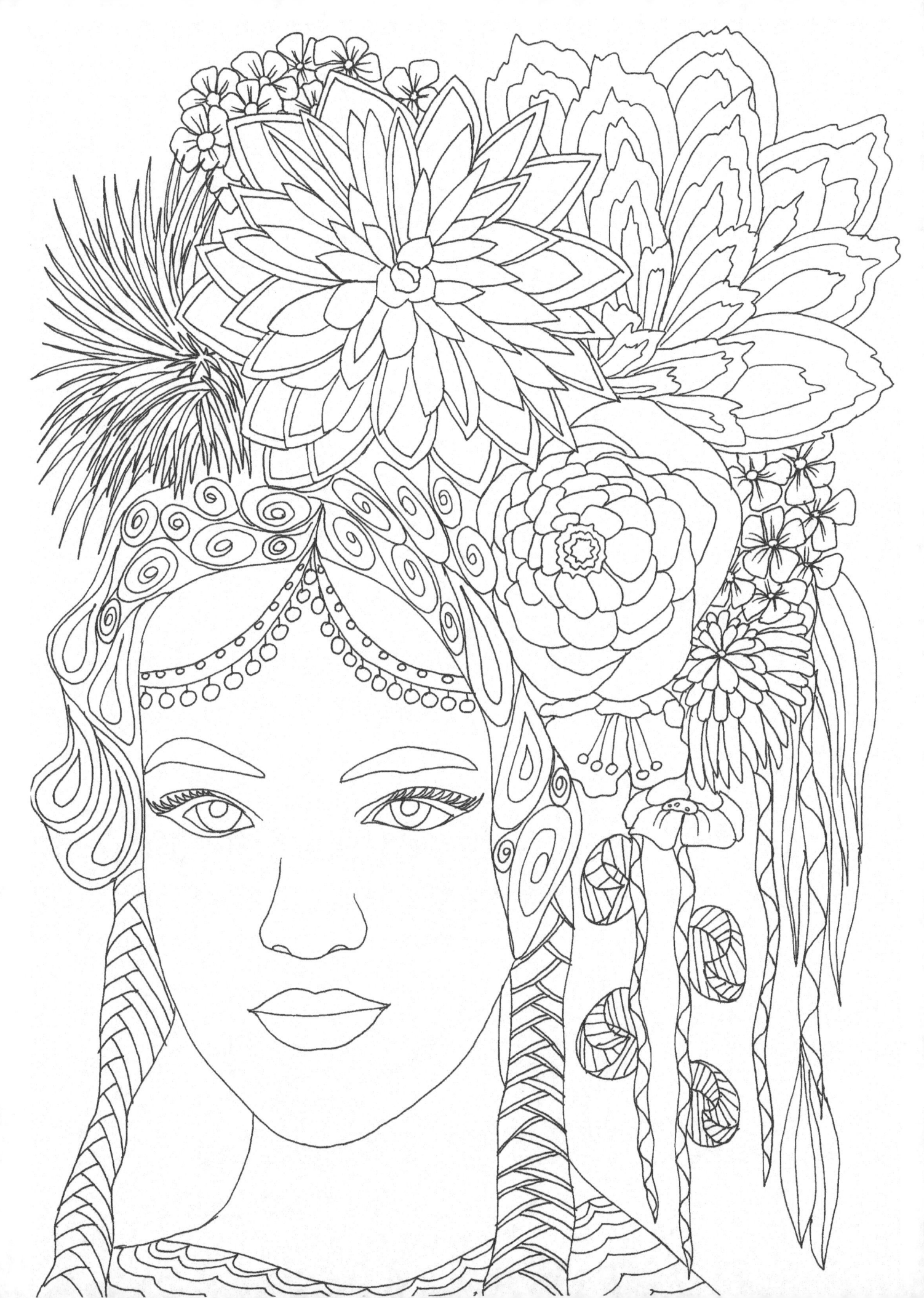

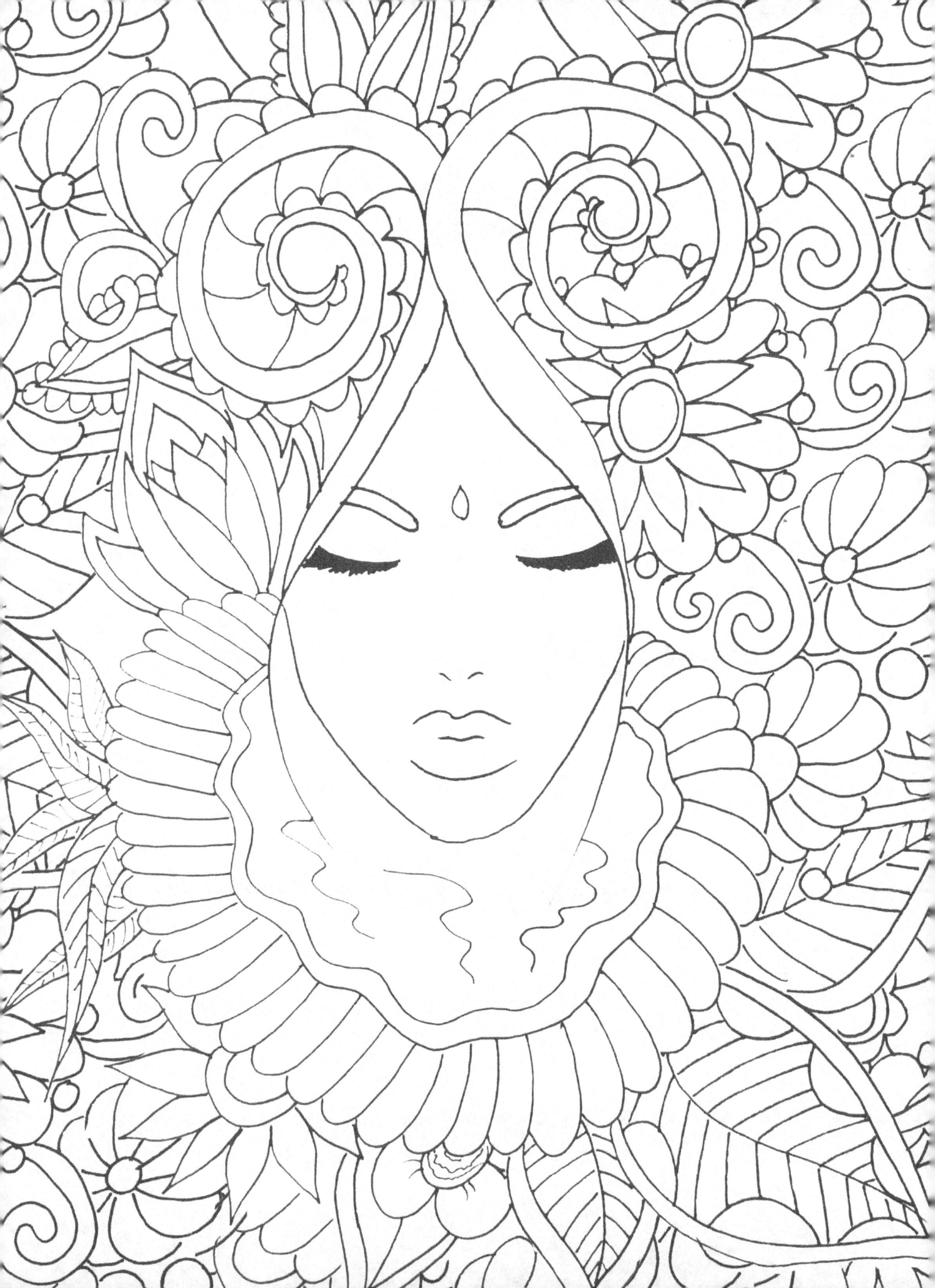

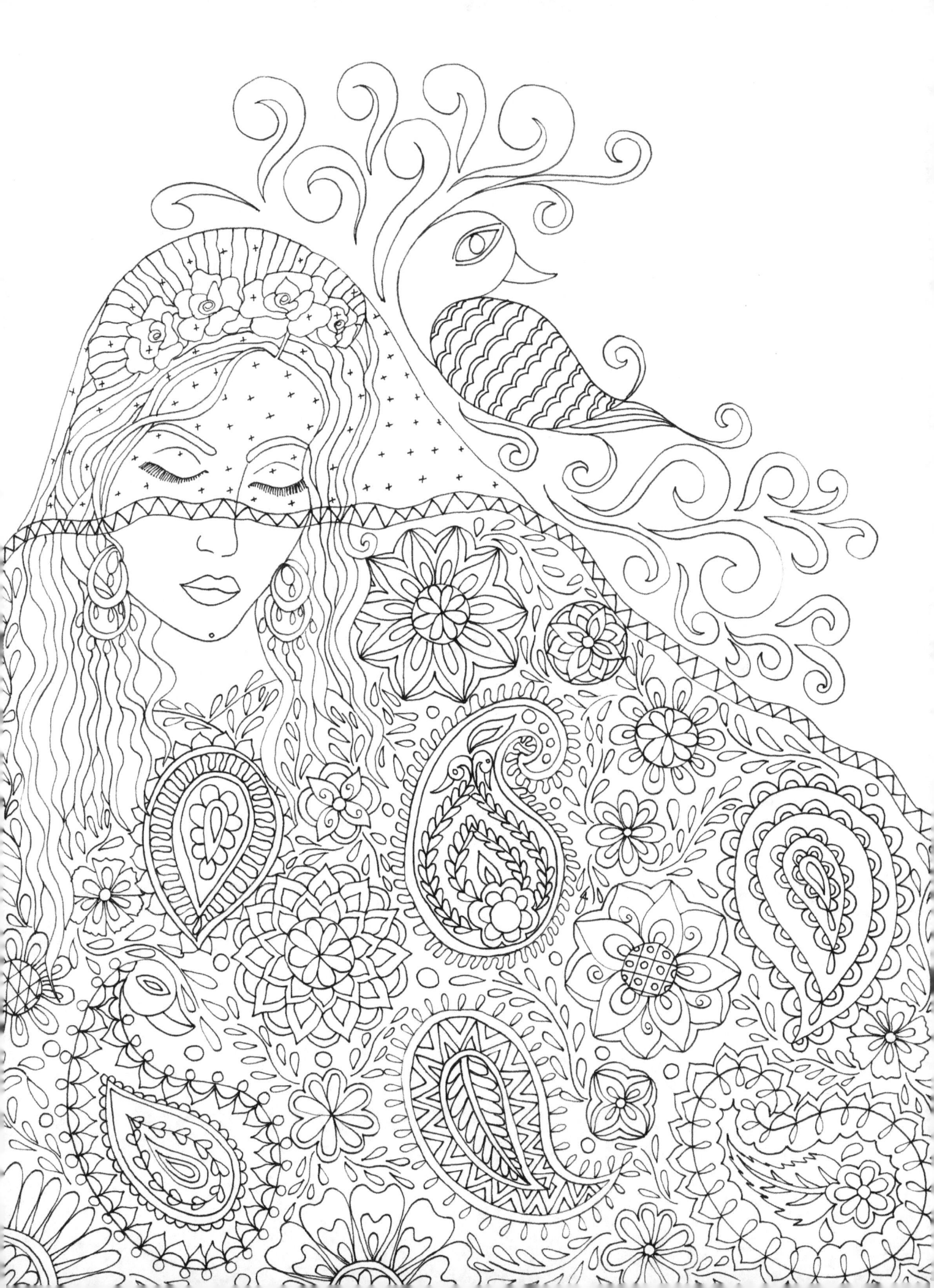

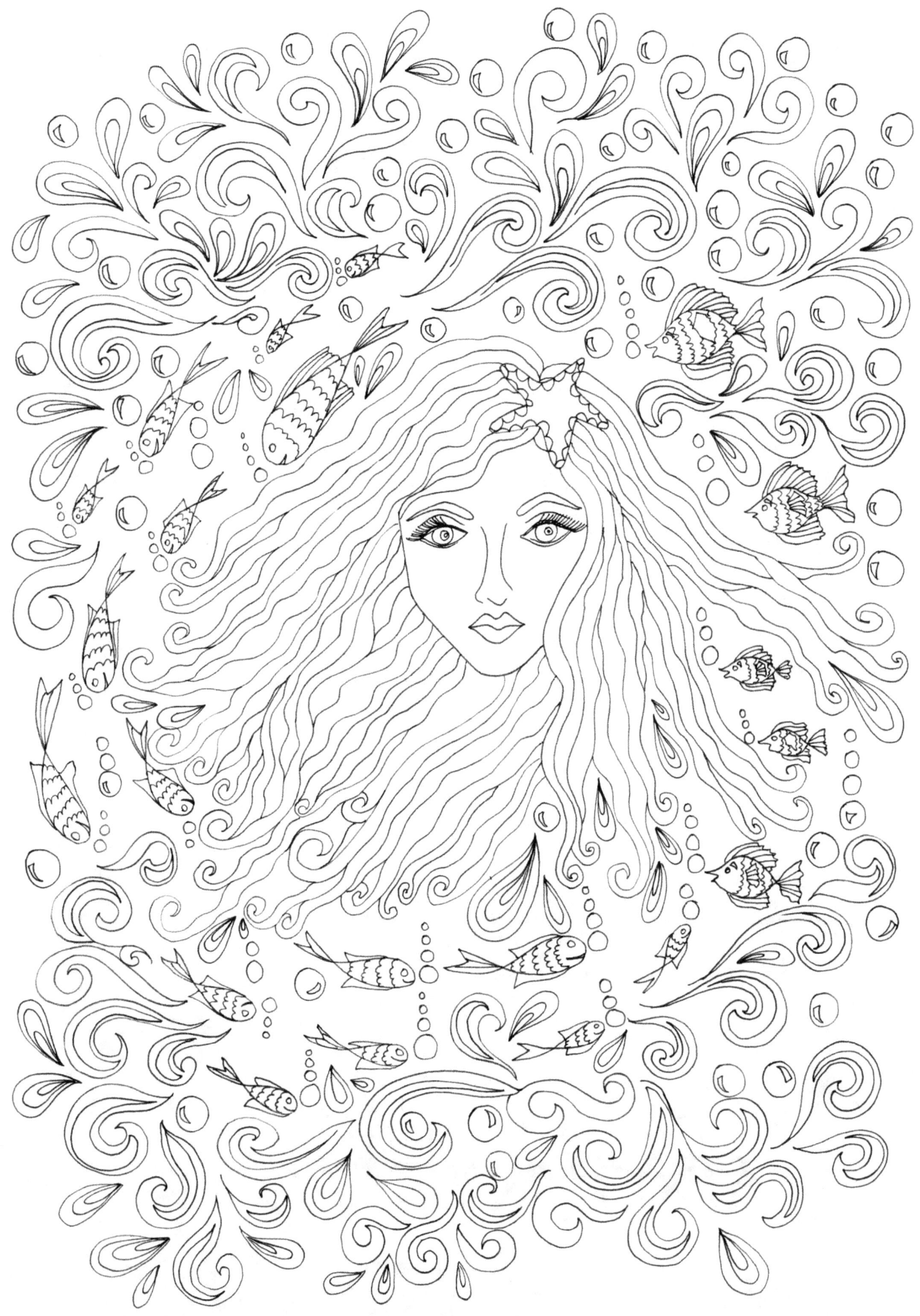

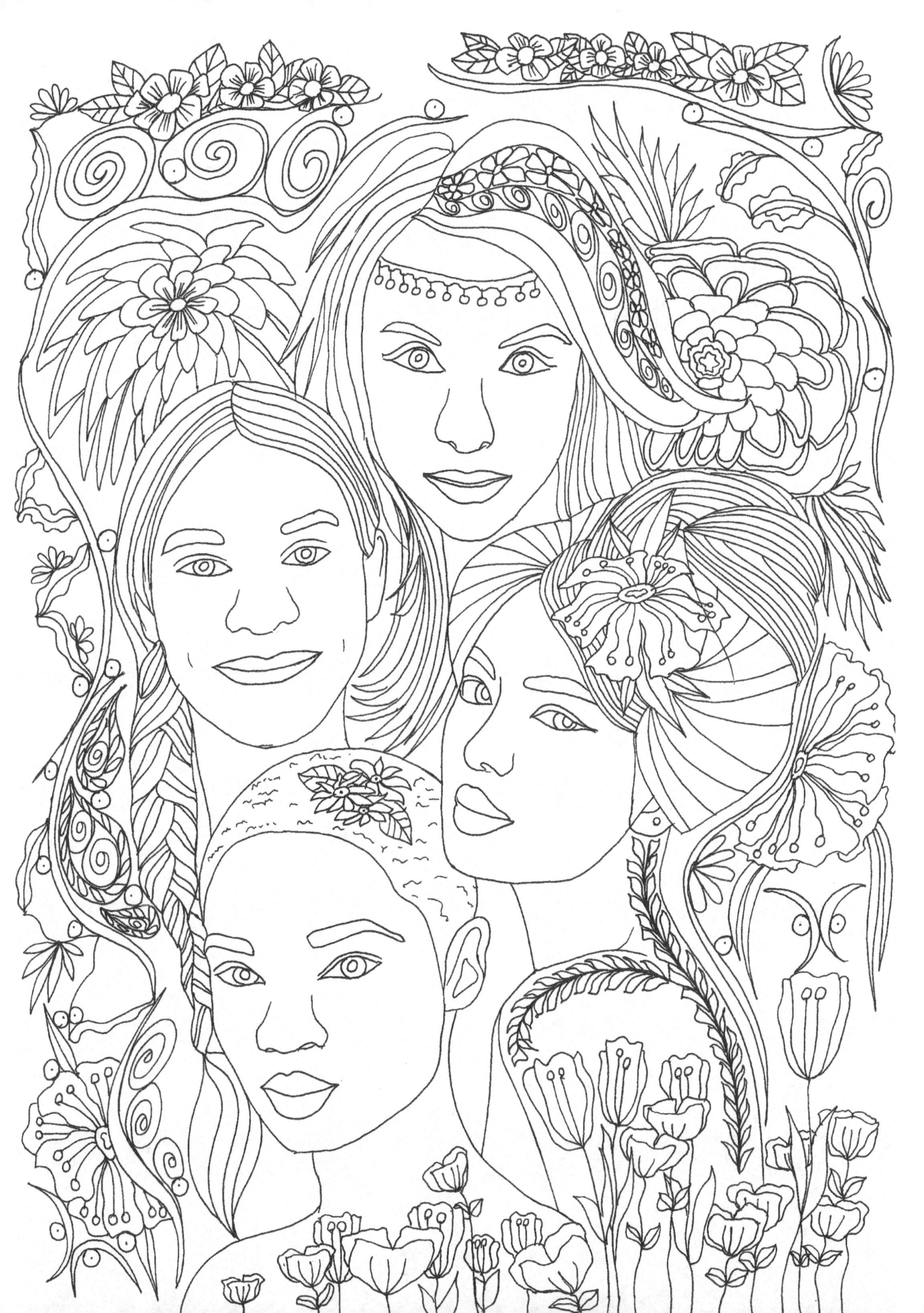

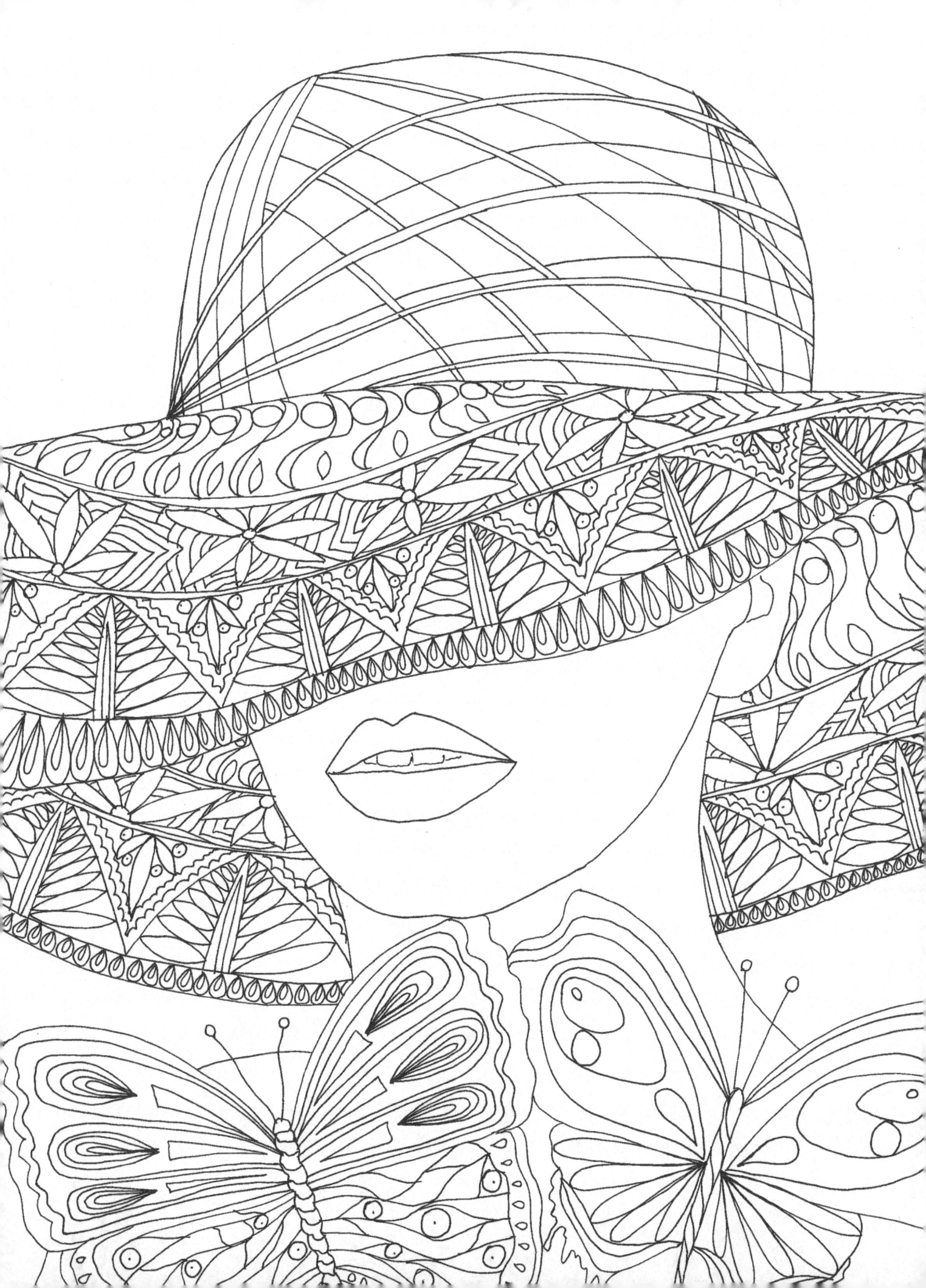

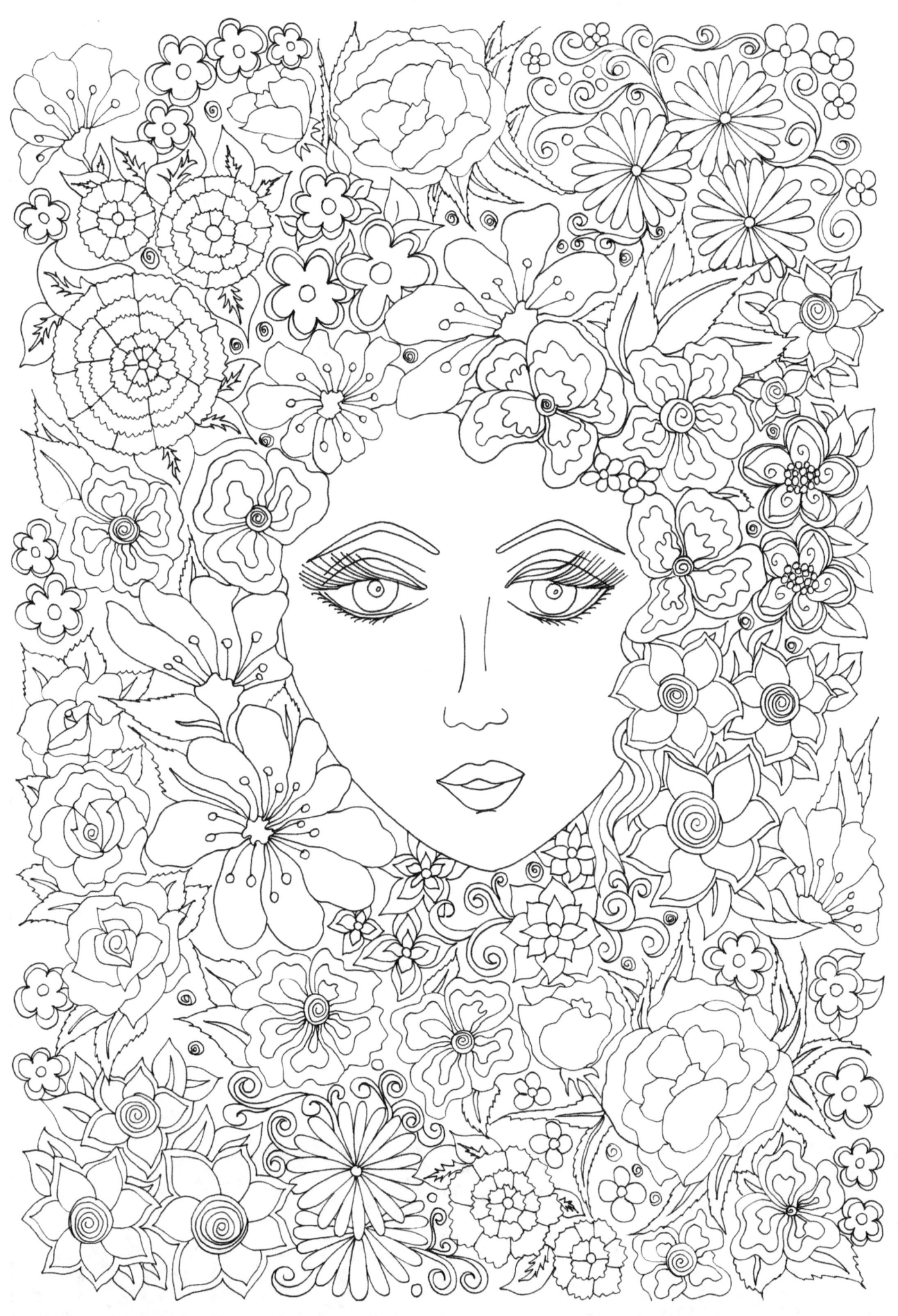

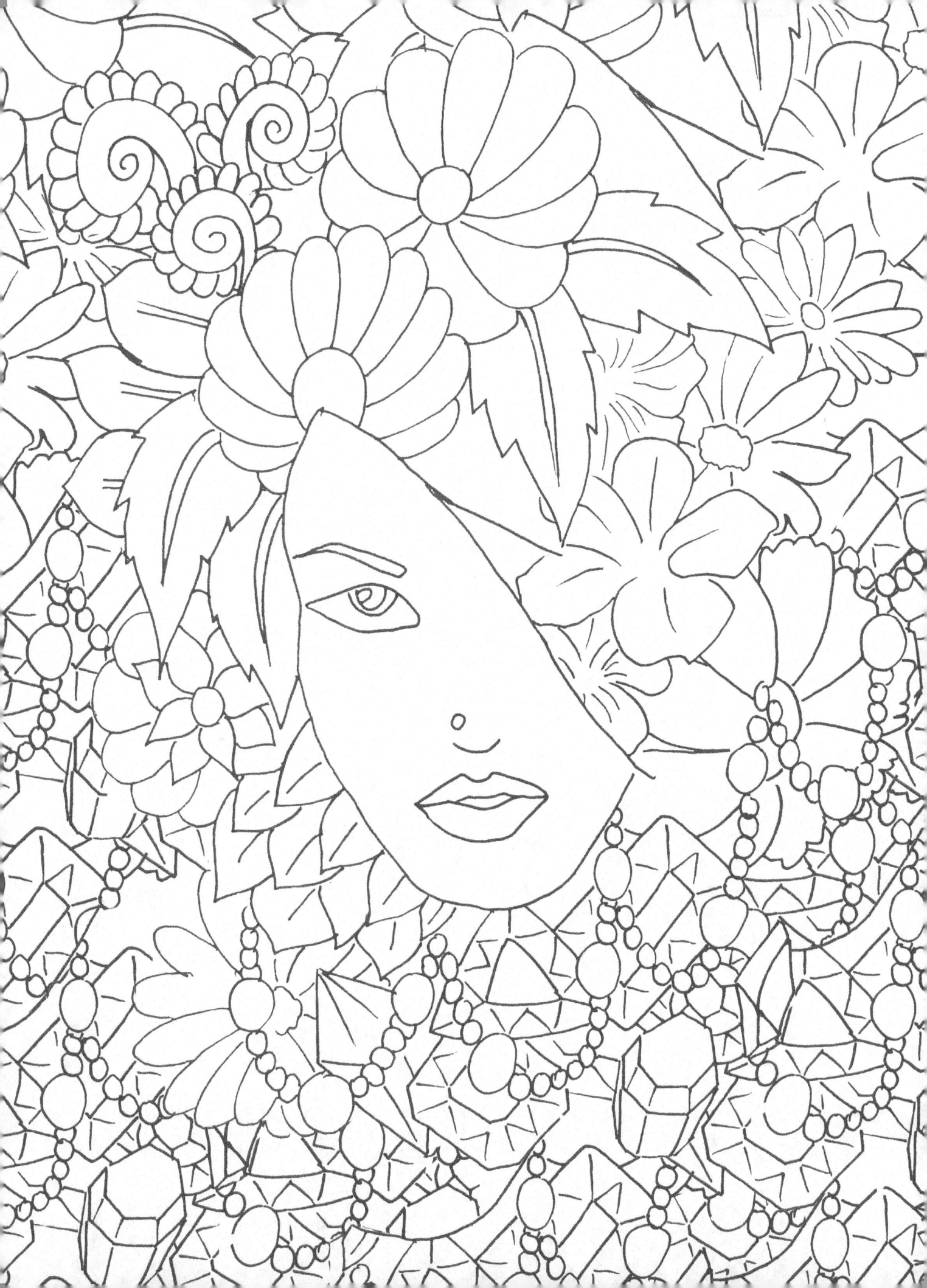

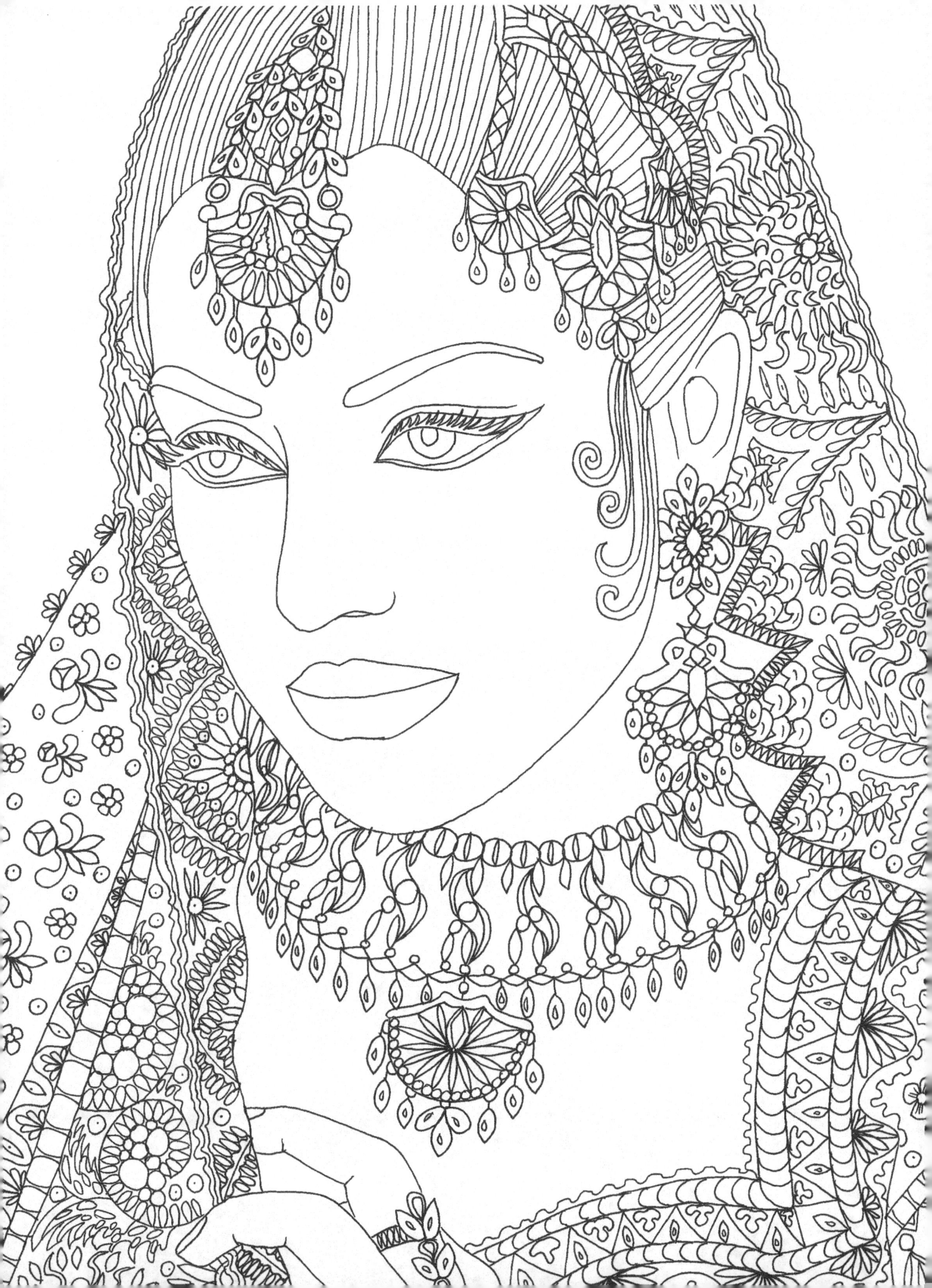

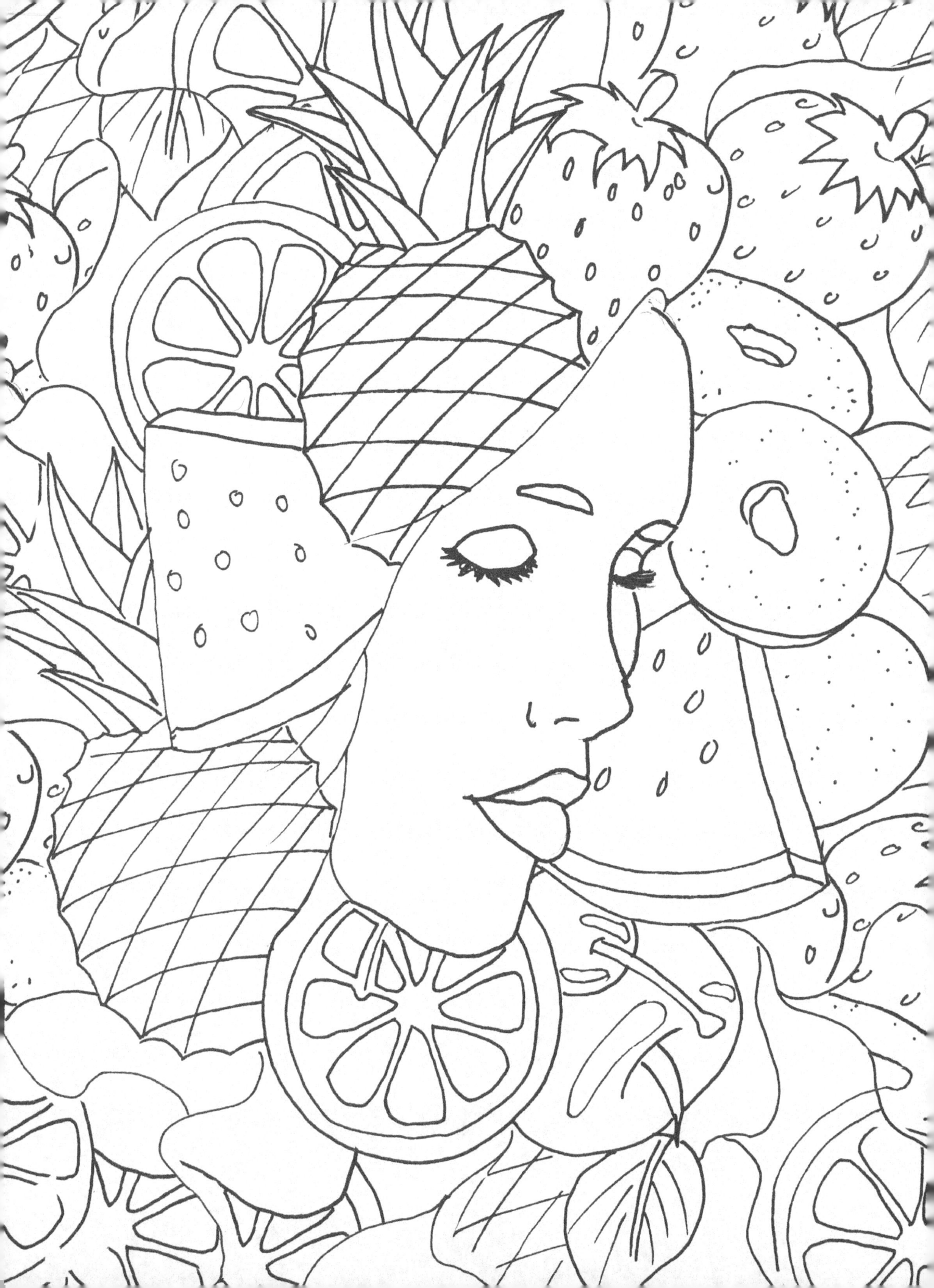

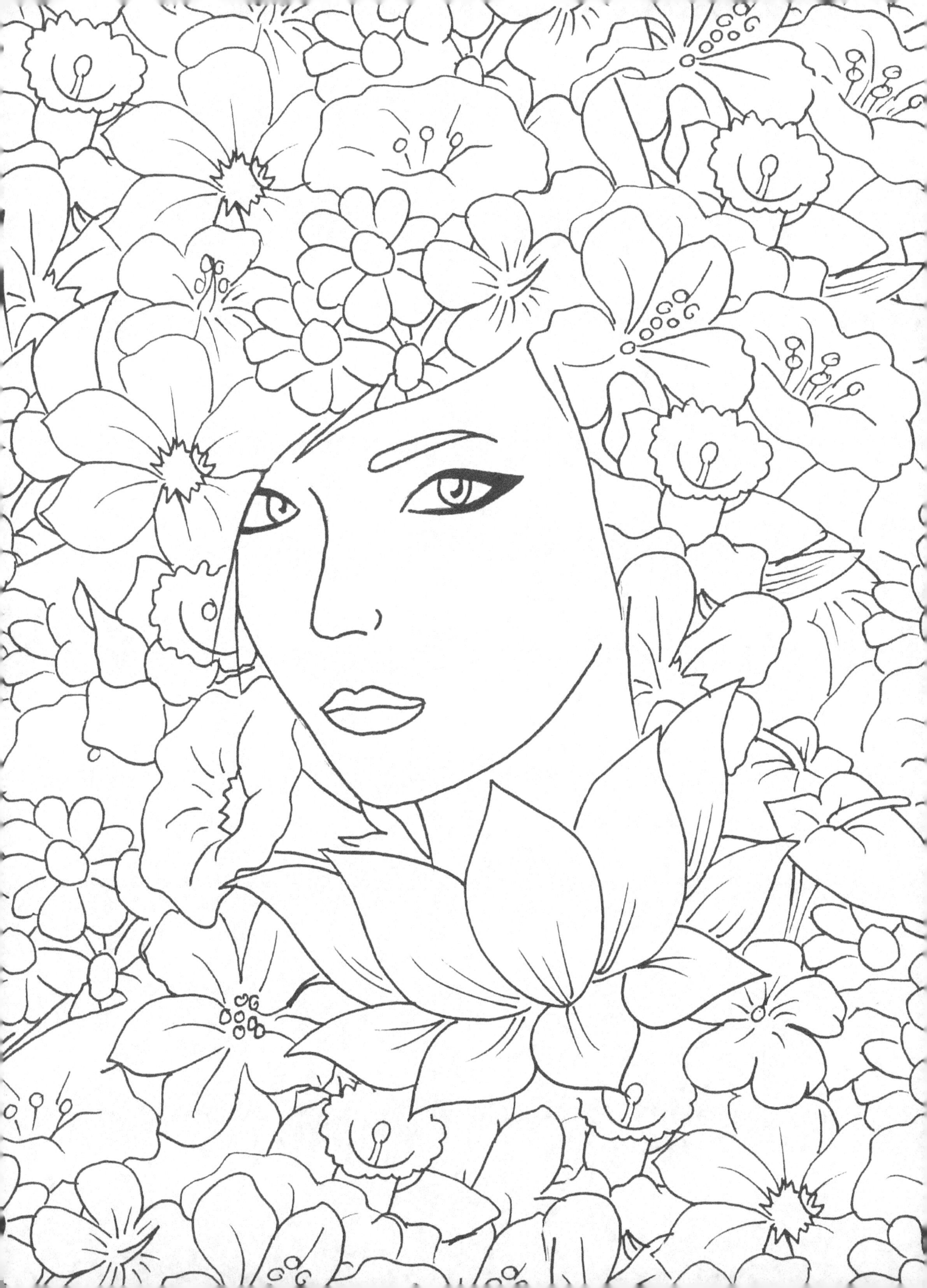

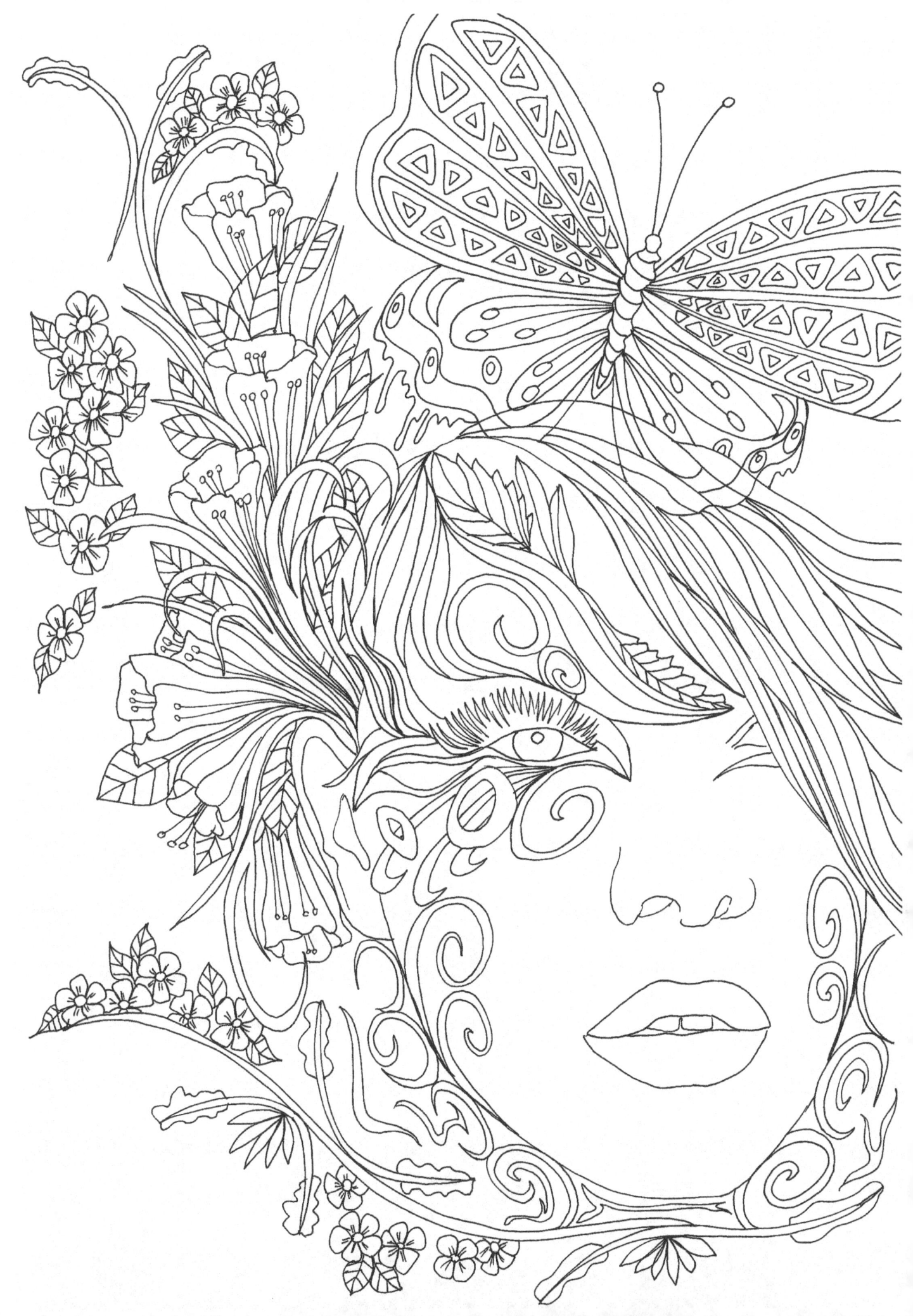

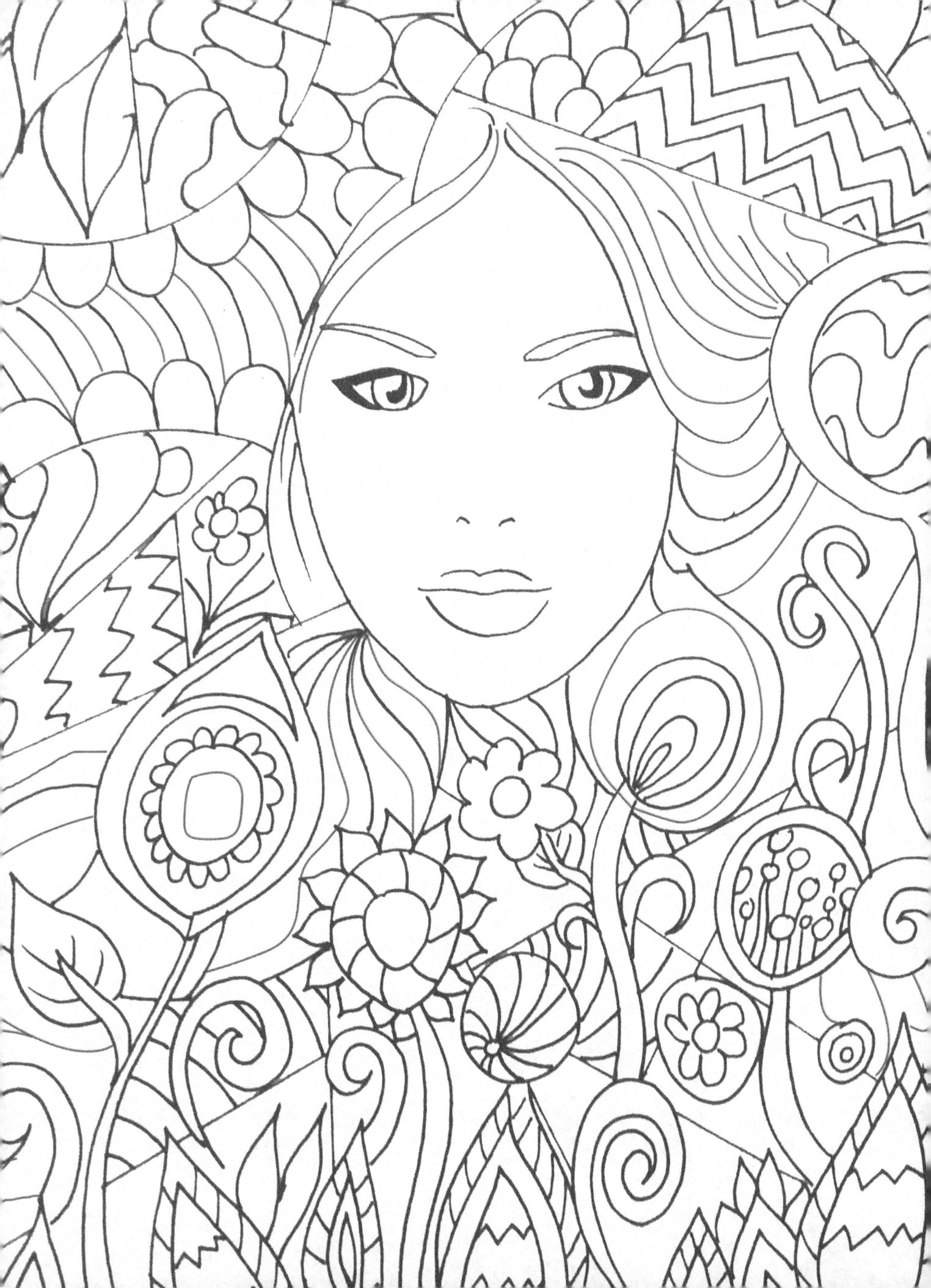

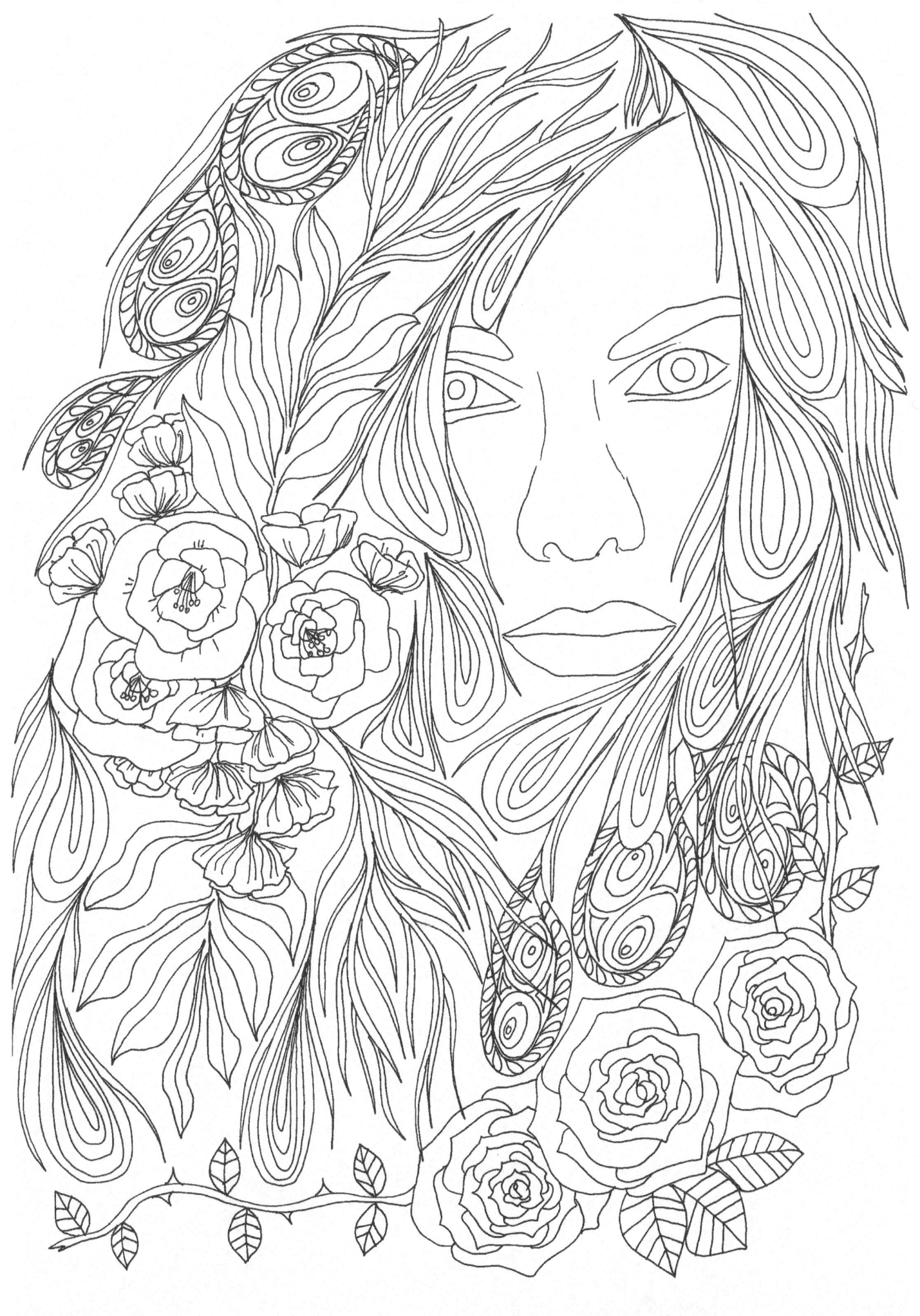

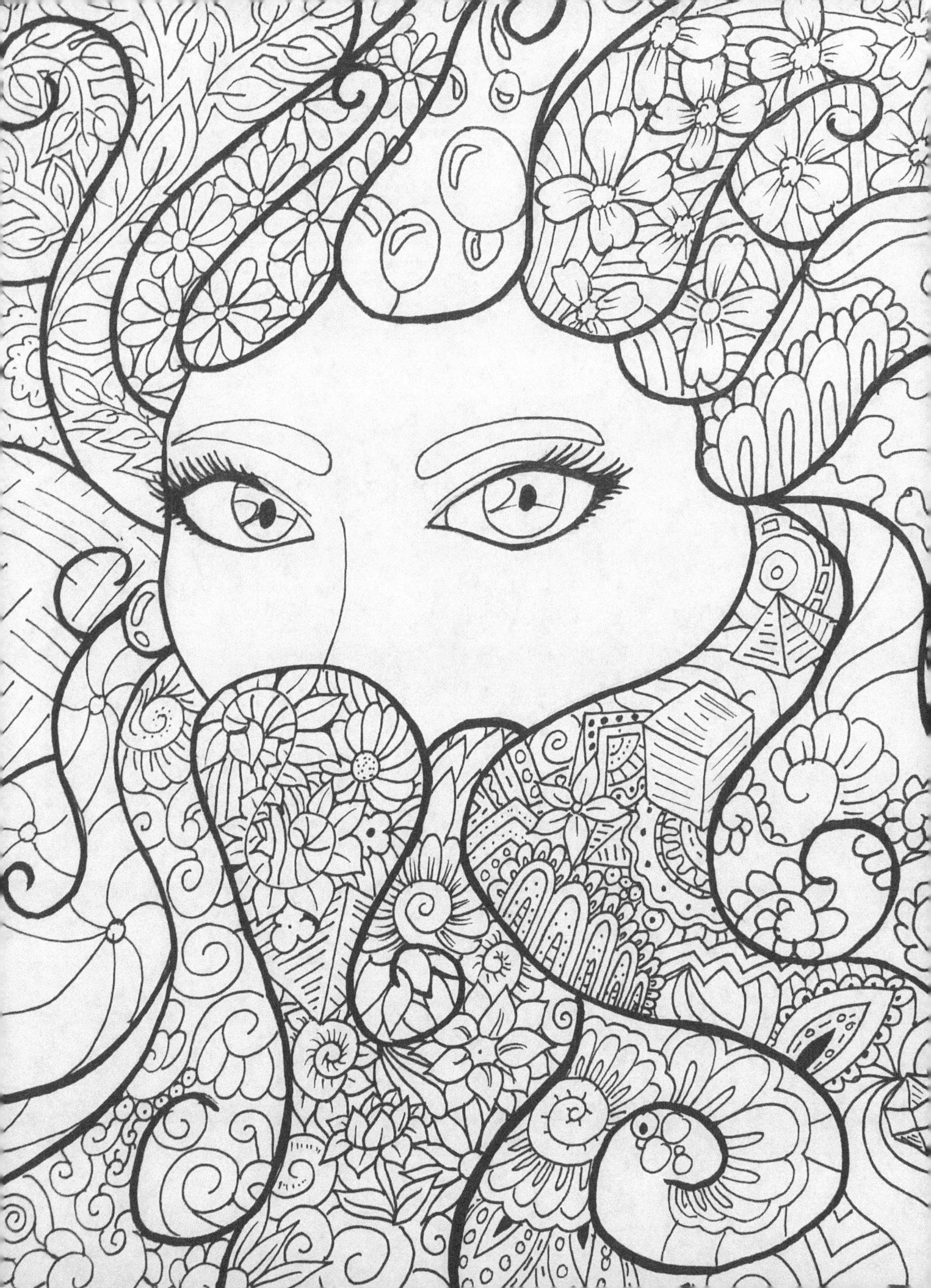

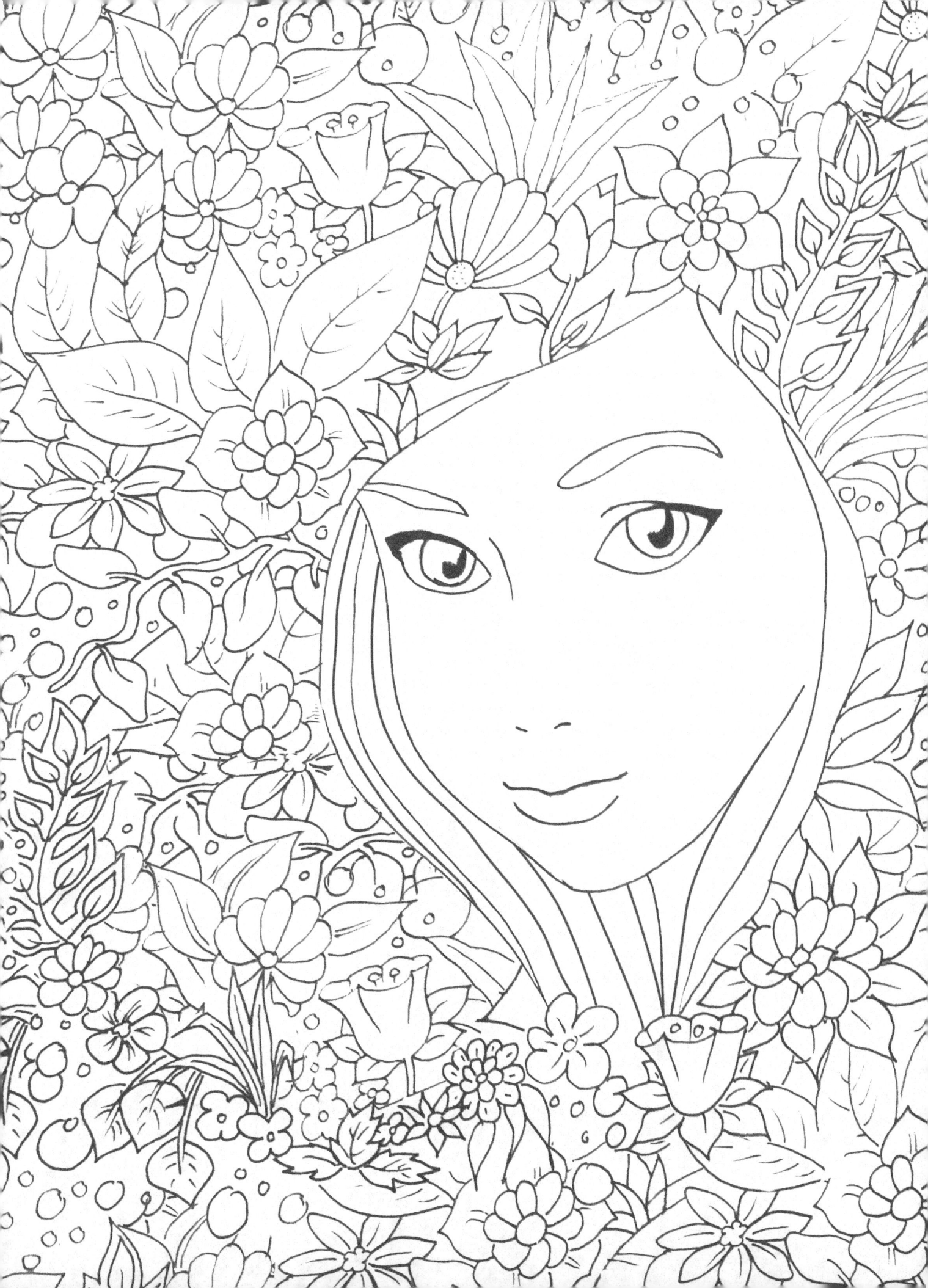

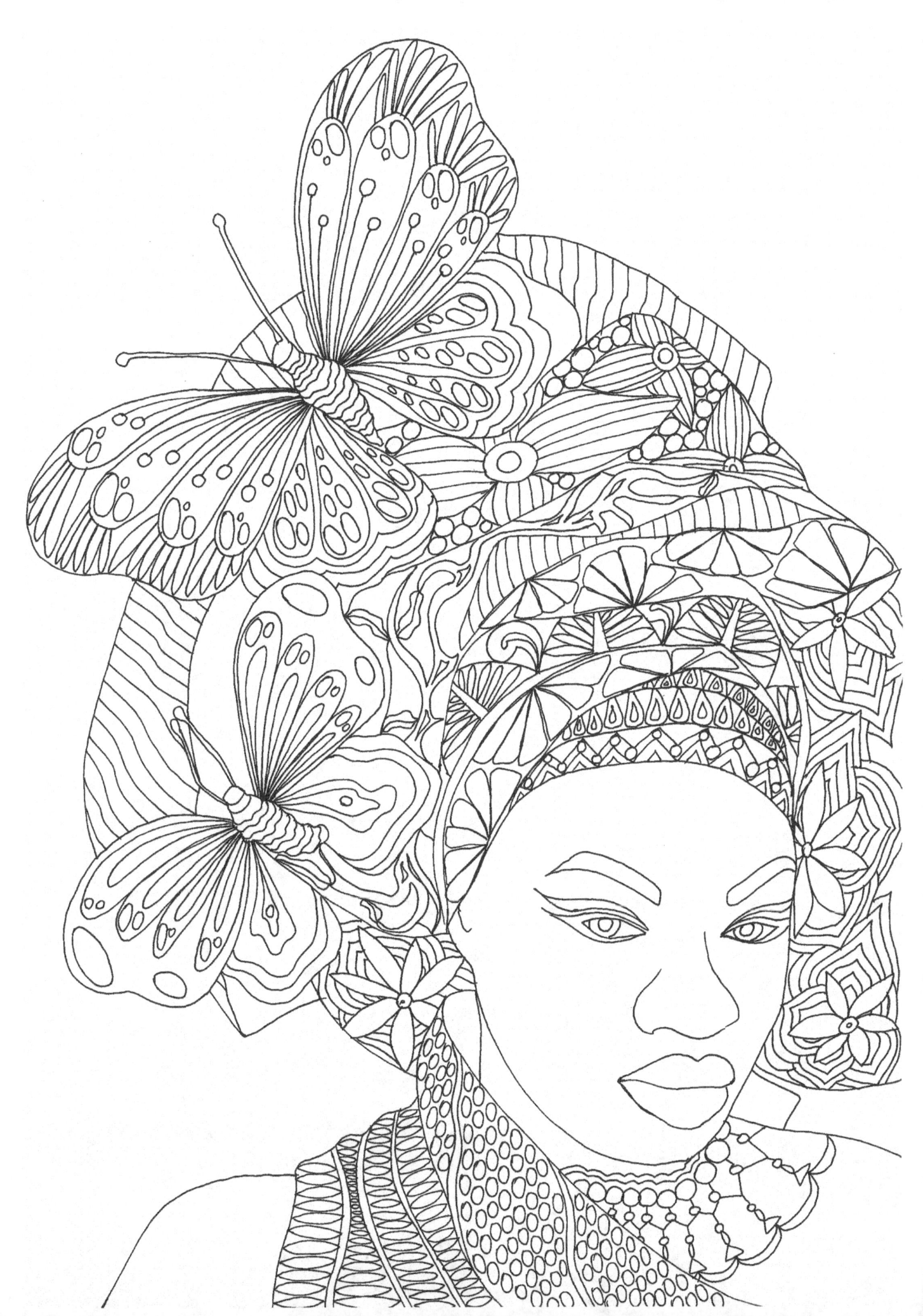

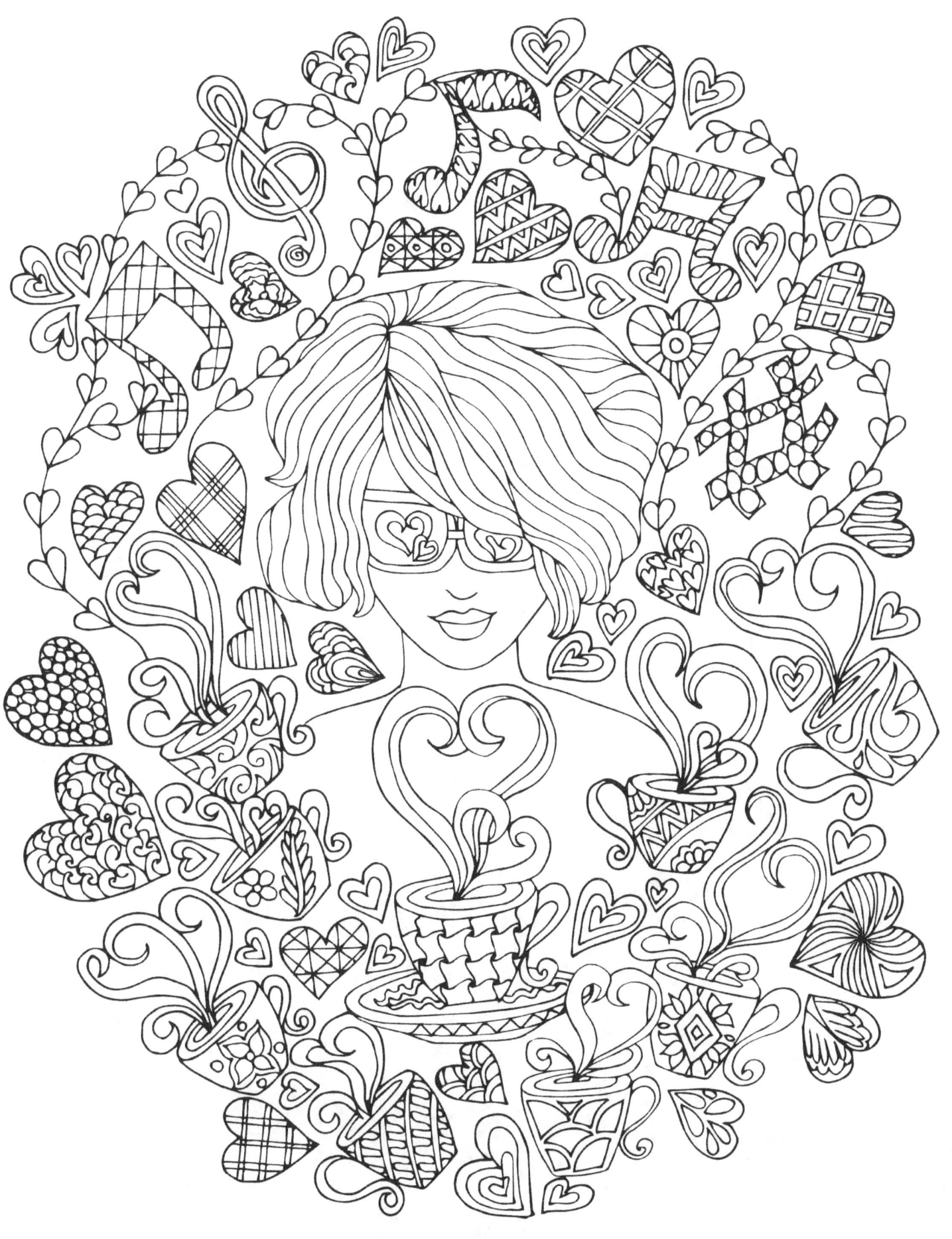

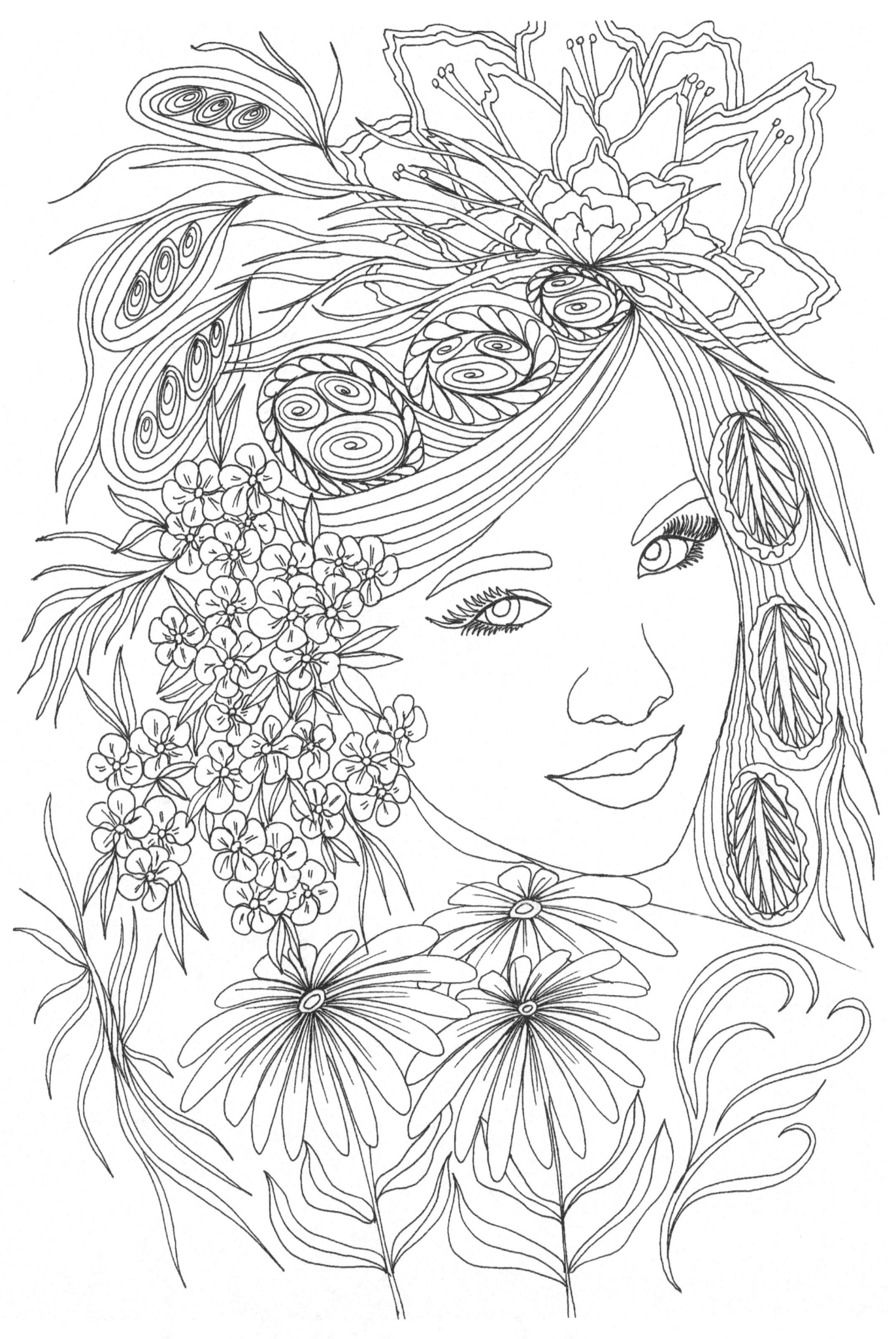

Be Happy Coloring Books

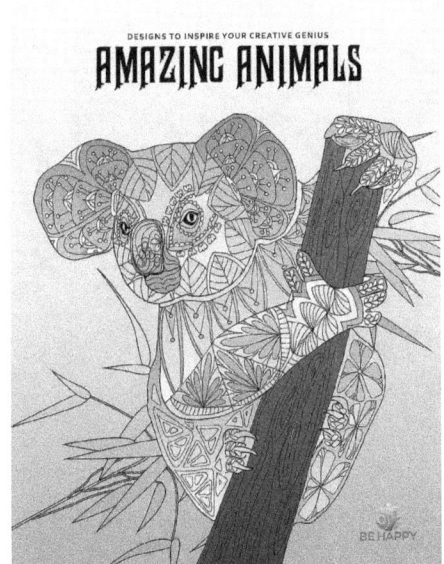
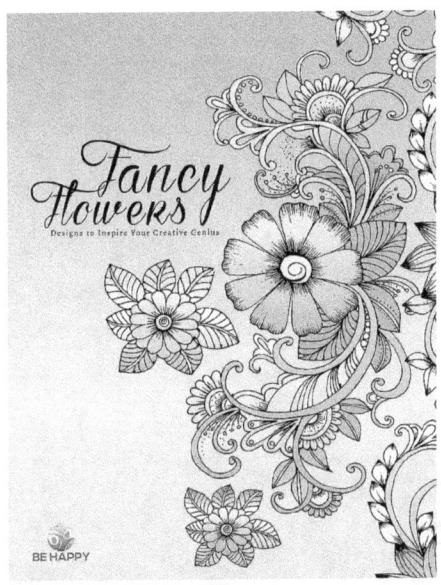
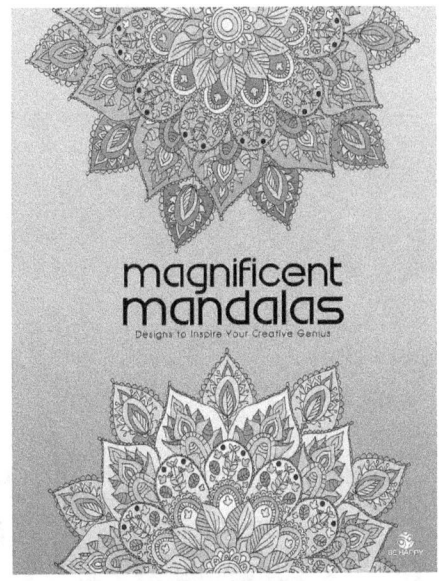
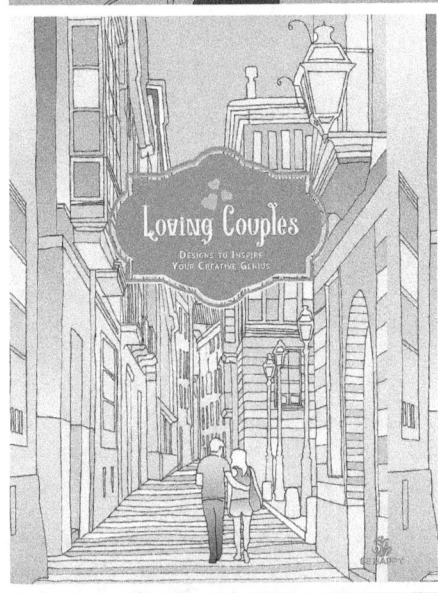
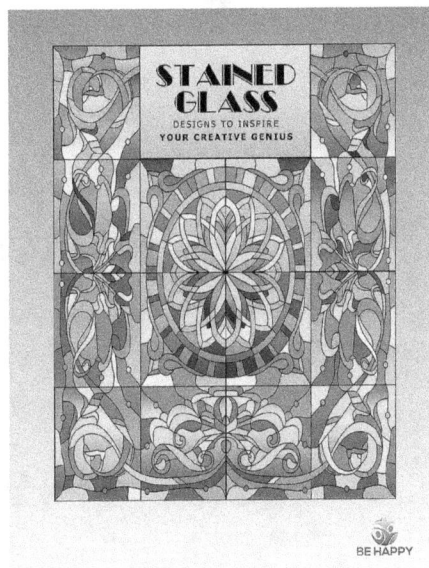
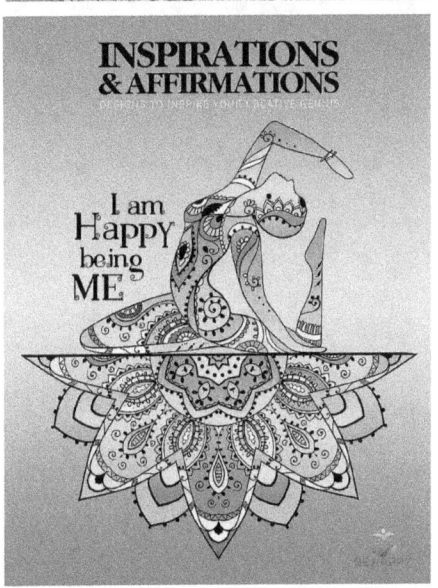
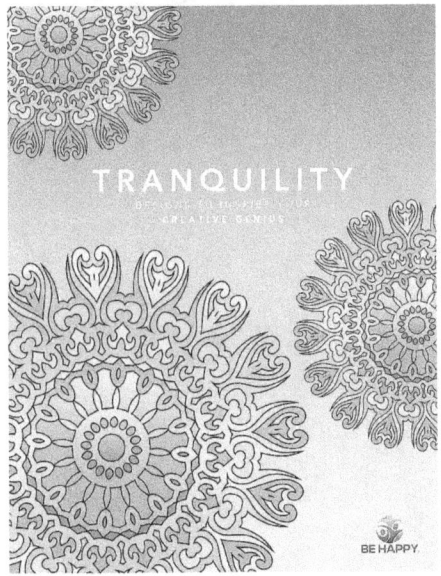